Robby Gallaty wakes up each ɪ
than that, he disciples people. H  pastor
who is deeply involved in making ⌐ɪpɪes. *Rediscover-*
ing Discipleship will be a helpful ⌐ tool for you.

> —**Eric Geiger,** Vice President at LifeWay Christian
> Resources

My friend Robby Gallaty has provided us with yet another tremendous resource for this all-important task of disciple-making. If you're interested in
returning to a Jesus-like model of discipleship, this book will point you in
the right direction. I learned a lot from it. I look forward both to studying it
with some of our key leaders, and to implementing several of the ideas in
our discipleship strategy.

> —**Tony Merida,** Pastor for Preaching and Vision, Imago
> Dei Church, Raleigh, NC; Associate Professor of
> Preaching, Southeastern Baptist Theological Seminary

If you are not careful when reading *Rediscovering Discipleship*, you may
forget you are reading a didactic book on discipleship and believe you are
enjoying an interesting romp through history. Dr. Gallaty has found a way
to make discipleship pleasurable. At the same time, the subject could not
be more important; it is about nothing less than world revolution. When
I take time to read on important subjects, I don't want to waste my time, I
want to read the best. I want experts who practice what they preach; Robby
Gallaty is such a man.

> —**Bill Hull,** Author of *Jesus Christ, Disciplemaker;*
> *The Disciple-Making Pastor; The Disciple-Making*
> *Church;* and more; founder of the Bonhoeffer Project

Robby's new book is both fresh and informational. You will enjoy his grasp
of the Jewish perspective on "discipling." I highly recommend this book …
both for discussion and personal interaction. It is simple, is practical, and
will stretch your understanding of Jesus and discipling. We must wrestle
with the issues that Robby raises in this book … the next generation of the
American church is at stake.

> —**Dr. Dann Spader,** Author of *4 Chair Discipling* and
> *Walking As Jesus Walked;* founder of Sonlife; President of
> Global Youth Initiative

Robby Gallaty has given pastors a prism that displays with brilliant color the bright white command to make disciples. You may never find a book with more clarity and conviction as it blends historic insight with present-day application.

— **WILL MANCINI,** Founder of Auxano,
author of *Church Unique*

Robby Gallaty's book is a manifesto for churches and Christians everywhere. God forbid, we spend our days succeeding at things that don't really matter in eternity. With loads of practical experience at the local church level, precision excellence, and masterful storytelling, Robby shows us the profoundly simple ways we can all make disciples like Christ. As one who loves to read, I really enjoyed Robby's writing.

— **MATT BROWN,** Evangelist, author of *Awakening*,
and founder of Think Eternity

Rediscovering Discipleship demonstrates why my friend, Robby Gallaty, is quickly becoming the most insightful, credible voice of this generation when it comes to disciple-making in the local church. This book confronts many of the shallow, popular notions of discipleship and provides a refreshing alternative that is thoroughly biblical and deeply practical. Every pastor and church leader desiring to create a church culture that will make mature, lasting disciples for Jesus must read this book.

— **BRIAN CROFT,** Senior Pastor, Auburndale Baptist Church,
Louisville, KY.; founder of Practical Shepherding; Senior
Fellow, Mathena Center for Church Revitalization,
SBTS

If you want a book filled with idealistic clichés or harsh critiques without practical solutions, this is NOT the book for you. But if you want to learn how to actually produce disciples in a modern-day church setting, I encourage you to let Robert Gallaty take you on a journey back through the disciplining methods of Jesus, the early church, and the Reformers as he highlights the transferable practices, principles, and methods of discipleship that still change lives today.

— **LARRY OSBORNE,** Author of *Sticky Church, Spirituality
for the Rest of Us*, and more; Pastor, North Coast Church,
San Diego County, Calif.

I love this book! Robby Gallaty has gifted the body of Christ with a compelling biblical and historical case for making disciples. I personally gleaned many new (or should I say "old") insights and stories from this dynamic, articulate, and wise pastor about the history, and hence the future, of disciple-making. Highly recommended!

— **Patrick Morley**, bestselling author,
and founder of Man in the Mirror

"Tell me how you keep score," former GE CEO Jack Welch said, "and I will tell you how to win." Not everything is easily measurable, but too many in the church have overly spiritualized discipleship to the point that measuring is not attempted at best or denigrated at worst. In this helpful book, Robby Gallaty offers the church cogent, clarifying tools for the journey of disciple-making. If you want to build a culture of disciples who make disciples, read this!

— **Alvin L. Reid**, Professor of Evangelism and Student
Ministry, Southeastern Baptist Theological Seminary

In *Rediscovering Discipleship*, Robby has given us a practical resource to aid believers in carrying out the Great Commission. Don't just read this book. Put it into practice.

— **Dr. Robert E. Coleman**, Author of
The Master Plan of Evangelism

There are little nuggets of gold to be found in this book, particularly when it comes to the practical side of discipleship. This will be a helpful tool for those looking to re-evaluate discipleship in the local church and how they can begin to "one another" more seriously in the faith.

— **Mez McConnell**, Senior Pastor of Niddrie
Community Church, Edinburgh, Scotland,
and Director of 20 Schemes

As Robby Gallaty puts it, "The lack of leadership isn't a leadership problem, it's a discipleship problem." This book, *Rediscovering Discipleship*, takes us back to Jesus' strategy to change the world and shows us how the greatest transformational movements in church history have always rediscovered the power of discipleship. In the swirling chaos of false substitutes, this book is a clarion call to authentic Christianity.

— **Byron Paulus**, President/Executive Director of Life
Action Ministries, Buchanan, MI

In *Rediscovering Discipleship*, Gallaty provides a necessary reminder that discipleship is not optional for Christians. Gallaty captures some of John Wesley's key insights about the importance of small group accountability for growth in holiness. This book contains practical insights and concrete steps for how to make disciples of Jesus Christ in local church contexts.

> —DR. KEVIN M. WATSON, Assistant Professor of Wesleyan
> and Methodist Studies at Candler School of Theology,
> Emory University

Reading *Rediscovering Discipleship* is like taking an antibiotic that fights off illnesses from overtaking the human body. This book is a healing agent that will help Jesus' body—the church—get healthy.

> —DERWIN L. GRAY, Lead Pastor, Transformation Church
> in South Carolina; author of *The High Definition Leader*

Robby Gallaty is not only a friend of mine, but an inspiration. As a senior pastor, I recognize how difficult it is to balance a crazy schedule and growing family in a way that still allows your "best" energy to go towards making disciples, and yet this is exactly what Robby is doing. He is not only writing and teaching on the subject; he's giving us a living, breathing model. I'm excited about *Rediscovering Discipleship* as an extension of Robby's example. I believe it will be useful in helping the church to return to its biblical calling, which is to make disciples who make disciples.

> —DR. KENNON VAUGHAN, Lead Pastor of Harvest Church,
> Germantown, TN; founder of Downline Ministries

Here is a practical "how to" book on discipleship written by a pastor who is passionate about "making the final words of Jesus our first work." I know of no one who is more effective in making disciples than Robby Gallaty. I wish I had had this book when I was beginning my ministry, because I realize it is not the number of sermons preached but the number of disciples made that really defines an effective ministry.

> —DR. ERWIN W. LUTZER, Senior Pastor,
> The Moody Church, Chicago

The heart of the Great Commission is about making disciples of Jesus Christ. In his book *Rediscovering Discipleship*, Robby Gallaty explains why the church needs to train and equip disciples, who in turn make disciples. With a proven strategy and a heart to grow the church, this book gives a simple process for accomplishing our mission mandate. If you are looking for a way to gauge the spiritual health and depth of your congregation, this book is for you.

— JACK GRAHAM, Pastor, Prestonwood Baptist Church in Texas

I have become convinced that the primary "shortage" in Great Commission work consists not of a lack of vision or a paucity of funds, but in the number of qualified disciple-makers our churches are producing. In this compelling and practical book, Robby returns us to Jesus' "Plan A" for reaching the world: "ordinary" Christians, filled with the Spirit, reproducing themselves wherever God places them. The future of the church lies not in flashier ministries or remarkable productions, but in reproducing disciples. Every church, of whatever size, can and should be involved in this crucial, and exhilarating, process.

— J.D. GREEAR, Ph.D., Lead Pastor of The Summit Church, Raleigh-Durham, N.C.; author of *Gaining by Losing* and *Jesus Continued...*

I'm excited! This is rich — it's not just another book on discipleship! It's a jewel that brings light, brilliance, beauty, and clarity to our understanding of discipleship, masterfully mined from the Hebrew setting of the Great "Co-mission." Discipleship is a "hot topic." Many are writing on it. However, *Rediscovering Discipleship*, I believe, lives up to its title. It will help you understand "discipleship," not as a spiritual wave, a fad of our times; rather, it's God's plan from the beginning, and this is how to get on with it according to the Word of God — which is our passion.

— KAY ARTHUR, Cofounder of Precept Ministries International; coauthor of the 40 Minute Bible Studies, *Being a Disciple: Counting the Real Cost*

Rediscovering Discipleship is the most helpful material on discipleship I have ever read. I do not know another area more critical for the church today, and Robby Gallaty has given us a tremendous tool to help us achieve what God has called us to do — make disciples.

— DR. MAC BRUNSON, Senior Pastor, First Baptist Jacksonville

Rediscovering
DISCIPLESHIP

MAKING JESUS' FINAL WORDS OUR FIRST WORK

ROBBY GALLATY

ZONDERVAN

Rediscovering Discipleship
Copyright © 2015 by Robert Gallaty

This title is also available as a Zondervan ebook. Visit www.zondervan.com/ebooks.

Requests for information should be addressed to:
Zondervan, 3900 *Sparks Dr. SE, Grand Rapids, Michigan 49546*

Library of Congress Cataloging-in-Publication Data

Gallaty, Robby, 1976-
    Rediscovering discipleship : making Jesus' final words our first work / Robby Gallaty.
      pages cm
    Includes bibliographical references.
    ISBN 978-0-310-52128-0 (softcover)
    1. Discipling (Christianity) 2. Missions. 3. Great Commission (Bible) I. Title.
    BV4520.G35 2015
    253 — dc23   2015011882

Published in association with the literary agency of Mark Sweeney & Associates, Bonita Springs, Florida 34135.

Cover design: Jared Challais
Cover art: © sergo/www.23RF.com
Interior design: Denise Froehlich

Printed in the United States of America

15 16 17 18 19 20 /DCI/ 20 19 18 17 16 15 14 13 12 11 10 9 8 7 6 5 4 3 2 1

To Kandi

*The way you selflessly motivate everyone around
you to grow closer to Jesus is
contagious. I am a better husband, father,
pastor, and disciple-maker because of you.
I am privileged to call you my wife, and our boys
are blessed to call you their mom.*

Contents

Foreword

WHY ARE SO MANY PEOPLE not growing deeper in their relationship with God?

The Bible tells us that we should be conscious of ourselves and of our teaching. Paul instructs Timothy, "Practice these things; be committed to them, so that your progress may be evident to all" (1 Tim. 4:15). In other words, it matters how you are growing and how *you're leading* your people to grow.

I believe that we would see more fruitful discipleship in our churches if we were to start by questioning our own spiritual formation before we question the development of those we lead and disciple. Are we seeking God in prayer, spending time in his Word, and surrounding ourselves with people who will challenge us to grow in our spiritual lives? Transformational discipleship involves moving from being in proximity to one another to being in community with one another. And it starts with you and with me.

When Eric Geiger and I were writing our book *Transformational Groups*, we did a study of 2,300 churches sponsored by 15 denominations. Less than half of those churches said they had any plan in place for discipling people, and only 60 percent had anyone *responsible for any level of spiritual formation among children, students, and adults.*

Soon afterward, we did a discipleship study called the Transformational Discipleship Assessment that studied more than 4,000 Protestant churchgoers and asked them about spiritual formation. Over the past few years, we've learned that:

- 41% of American Protestant churchgoers do not attend small classes or groups from their churches.
- 42% of American Protestant churchgoers intentionally spend time with other believers in order to help them grow in their faith.
- 54% of American Protestant churchgoers say they set aside time daily to a few times a week for private worship, praise or thanksgiving to God (prayer not included).
- 25% of American Protestant churchgoers say they have shared their faith once or twice; 14% have shared three or more times over the last six months.
- 19% of American Protestant churchgoers read the Bible every day.

Based on the results of the study, we were able to identify eight "attributes of discipleship" that consistently show up in the life of a maturing Christian: Bible engagement, obeying God and denying self, serving God and others, sharing Christ, exercising faith, seeking God, building relationships, and unashamed transparency. Our conclusion: God shapes congregations through the shaping of the individual lives of people. And this shaping doesn't just happen randomly. God grows us as *we place ourselves in a position of obedience to receive that growth.*

Today, there is a "discipleship deficit" in the church. Upon hearing about this, more than one concerned leader has asked us, "What should we do?" and "How should we do it?" These leaders want to know the best ways to turn this deficit into a culture of robust discipleship.

That's where a book like *Rediscovering Discipleship* comes in. In this book, Robby Gallaty writes about how the Great Commission must impact the way we discuss and engage in discipleship in our churches.

In part one, Robby outlines the need to know the man, Jesus, before you go on his mission. This is *crucial*. Too many of us are so focused on what we're supposed to do for Jesus that we lose focus on Jesus himself. Robby spends a great deal of time and energy outlining Jesus and his methods so that we do not forget about the Man who sends us on the mission. In part two, Robby dives deep into specific methods of discipleship, showing how the church can effectively make disciples in order to live on the mission Christ has for us.

Robby is a great thinker, and he lays out helpful, practical, and realistic strategies that local churches can implement to multiply disciples who live on mission in their everyday lives.

Today, we need to once again rediscover discipleship—and Robby points us in the direction to do that in the way Jesus modeled and directed for us.

—Ed Stetzer,
author of *Subversive Kingdom*,
www.edstetzer.com

Introduction

ANYTHING OLD IS OLD-FASHIONED TO much of the Western world. However, two movements that altered the course of human history were the Renaissance (1300–1700) and the Reformation (1500–1600), both of which recovered or rediscovered what was lost. By looking into the past, they were able to take giant strides forward.

A return to discipleship will enact the reformation of the twenty-first century. The strategy is not new. The method has been time-tested and is culturally relevant in any context. Discipleship works as well in a small, rural church as it does in a major city megachurch. A seasoned pastor can experience the same results as an inexperienced minister. Laymen without seminary education or years of ministerial experience are able to reach the nations by implementing these core discipleship principles.

Yet my driving motive for writing this book is not to raise the banner of discipleship; it's a clarion call for cultivating a deeper walk with Christ. I am passionate about disciple-making because my desire is to obey Jesus. When a person grows closer to him, the yield will be discipleship.

Discipleship is effective because it empowers believers to shoulder the work of ministry. Every individual in a discipleship ministry has another person they are working with. Disciples, many for the first time, are equipped to take *responsibility* for their faith and *ownership* for their God-given ministries. We are here because the first disciples took Jesus at his word. They made

Jesus' last words their first work. What would happen if we did the same? I believe we would rediscover what it means to be a New Testament church.

The Greatness of the Great Commission

What makes the Great Commission so "great"? It is that small two-letter prefix "co-." Jesus could have told us about the Great Mission, something he would do alone. Instead, he enlisted us to join him in what we call the Great Co-Mission. As believers, we cooperate with him in a synergistic manner — working together.

In his book *WikiChurch*, Steve Murrell tells the story of a ten-year-old judo student who was seriously injured in a car accident. The student's arm was so badly injured that the doctors were left with no choice but to amputate it. Everyone thought his judo career was over, yet despite his handicap, he persevered and continued his training. His teacher, aware of a plan the boy didn't yet understand, taught him one move and one move only. The boy petitioned his teacher every day to teach him more than one technique, but the teacher would not change his mind. Every day of every week of every month was spent perfecting this one move.

The boy entered his first tournament after the injury and, against all odds, advanced to the finals. His opponent in the finals was more seasoned, faster, stronger, and, as was immediately apparent, in possession of all of his limbs. The match was a stalemate until the seasoned competitor lost focus for a moment. The one-armed boy performed the only major move he knew, and his opponent could do nothing to counter it. To everyone's surprise, the one-armed boy was crowned the champion.

According to Murrell, the one-armed student won the match for two simple reasons: "First of all, he has mastered one of the most difficult moves in all of judo. Second, the only defense against that move is to grab your opponent's left arm."[1] Although I cannot confirm if this story is true, it still communicates a principle we must all learn: simplify. Learn to keep the main thing the main thing. When we do this and stop majoring on the minors, we become far more effective in our ministry efforts. Until disciple-making becomes *the* ministry of the church and not *a* ministry in the church, we will never see our discipleship efforts impact the world the way that Jesus envisioned.

This generation, as with every generation, has a fresh opportunity to reclaim this ancient pattern of ministry. Today's church leaders are not like the generations immediately preceding them. Church in a box is outdated like Cavaricci jeans (you only know about these if you're older than thirty), canned sermons are frowned upon, and more leaders understand their need for a comprehensive disciple-making strategy — the crux of the Great Commission. What is missing from the equation, unfortunately, is a measurable method for tracking effectiveness.

BirthMARCS of a D-Group

"Create incarnational principles, not duplicatable processes for people to implement," was the advice of Will Mancini, author and visionary, in an hour-long phone conversation I had with him about disciple-making.[2] Mancini is talking here about a common phenomenon among ministry leaders. Many churches will experience success in a particular area of ministry and then attempt to repackage a step-by-step process for duplication in other churches. In the 1990s, many churches adopted the "Purpose Driven" model for ministry, which was very effective at the time.[3]

But after years of implementing it as a nicely packaged, sure-fire disciple-making strategy, it began to fade. And some of this is due to the need to contextualize each strategy to our local culture. What works in Chattanooga, Tennessee, may not work in San Francisco or in Quito, Ecuador. The Word of God and the principles it teaches are timeless and transcendent, but man-made curriculums developed in a particular cultural context are not.

When God determines the maturity of a church, he doesn't *count* the Christians — he weighs them, and the weight is measured by how deeply his teaching has penetrated into a person's life. *Depth* is more important than *width*; the transformation of a single person can have a greater impact than hundreds of shallow commitments. And as we will discover later, Jesus instituted this principle in his own disciple-making ministry. His plan for reaching the world was not through massive evangelism conferences, though they have their place, but by investing in people who would then invest themselves in discipling others.

Depth is a hard thing to measure, is it not? How do you measure the maturity of an individual? Are there certain elements that are essential for determining whether or not a discipleship group (D-Group) is healthy? I believe that there are. We will unpack these elements in later chapters, but here I want to introduce you to the MARCS of a healthy discipleship group. The MARCS are as follows:

- Missional
- Accountable
- Reproducible
- Communal
- Scriptural

In chapter 13 we will examine each of these five categories more closely. And by the end of this book you will not only have a fresh appreciation for the ancient practice of discipleship, but also will have learned how to develop a comprehensive discipleship system that will serve as the guide rails for implementing a new discipleship ministry … or for fine-tuning your existing one.

Redefining Success

Imagine that you are asked to keep score of a football game for a local high school. You arrive early at the field, make your way to the press box, and prepare to document touchdowns and turnovers. But you immediately notice a problem: you forgot to bring a scorecard. You search your pockets and find that all hope is not lost. You still have an unused scoring card from a round of golf you played earlier. What luck!

Shortly into the first quarter, the home team scores the opening points. You ask the official in the booth next to you, "What did they shoot?"

"What did they shoot?" he replies to you, somewhat quizzically. "The team scored a touchdown and made the extra point for a total of seven points."

You write down a seven, which is three strokes above the allotted par of four for the first hole. As you can imagine, you'll quickly find out that you cannot record football stats on a golf scorecard. In the same way, we cannot judge church success by the standards of another model.

Many church leaders today easily fall into the trap of gauging success in the church by the ABCs of growth: Attendance, Buildings, and Cash. However, there is a serious problem with this scorecard, namely, that *Jesus never gauged effectiveness by these criteria.*

Read the Gospels. Jesus didn't draw large crowds for the sake of counting heads or logging attendance. Although he did speak to the masses, he consistently left them to be in the close company of the twelve in his inner circle. Acts 1 records that after Jesus ascended into heaven, only 120 disciples gathered together to pray for God to empower them through his Spirit. This approach stands in stark contrast to most modern church growth standards of success. Jesus spoke with unprecedented authority. He raised the dead. He gave sight to the blind. He healed the sick. These miracles constantly drew increasingly large crowds, yet after his departure, only 120 people met to continue his work.

By referring to them as "only 120" I do not wish to discount the miraculous work of our Lord, but rather to point out that Jesus was not interested in expanding out at the expense of growing miles deep. Rather, he focused on developing mature, faithful disciples who carried a revolutionary directive: go make more of you. This does not mean that you should try and kill your church, only that numbers often give a false sense of accomplishment. So whether your church draws 50 or 50,000, depth is the goal.

We should also keep in mind that during his earthly ministry, Jesus never owned anything. The Bible tells us that he didn't even have a place to lay his head, much less a regular meeting place for his "congregation" (see Luke 9:58). The acquisition of buildings for meeting together was not a priority on his to-do list. Buildings are not evil, but they shouldn't be our primary model for trying to make disciples. Anyone can fill a building with people, but not everyone can make them into disciples.

Finally, it is good for us to remember that Jesus was not impressed with cash or finances. Yes, he taught on money more than on heaven and hell combined, but he never put much stock in the size of the traveling treasury. Again, this is not to say that a large or small ministry budget is good or bad — money allows most ministries to exist; rather, we must remember that it was not an ultimate focus of Jesus and should not be an ultimate focus of ours. Consider whom Jesus appointed to head up his ministry funds: Judas, who betrayed him for a meager thirty pieces of silver.

Multipliers

Jesus implemented a strategy of multiplication with the men he hand-selected, by leveraging the talents and abilities of each one. In the book *Multipliers*, authors Liz Wiseman and Greg McKeown describe the mentality of a multiplier:

> Instead of achieving linear growth by adding new resources, you can more efficiently extract the capability of your people and watch growth skyrocket. Leaders rooted in the logic of multiplication believe: 1. Most people in organizations are underutilized. 2. All capability can be leveraged with the right kind of leadership. 3. Therefore, intelligence and capability can be multiplied without requiring a bigger investment.[4]

Sound familiar? Jesus' discipleship ministry solidified this strategy. The authors go on to say,

> Multipliers don't necessarily get more with less. They get more by using more — more of people's intelligence and capability.

As one CEO put it, "Eighty people can either operate with the productivity of fifty or they can operate as though they were five hundred."[5]

Jesus used eleven men to change the world. You are reading this book today as a result of their ministries.

Closing the Revolving Back Door

If I am going to be completely transparent with you, I will admit to falling into this trap myself. Early in my ministry I would regularly challenge my members to invite their friends to church. Although I wouldn't have admitted this at the time, our invitation was more about us than about them. We weren't all that concerned about their personal needs, and as soon as they began attending we would encourage them to repeat this process with their friends. When those friends arrived, we extended to them the same charge to get *their* friends to church.

People would stick around for a few months, but many would eventually leave. Our church became a revolving door, with new people exiting the back faster than guests were walking through the entrance. Having talked with other pastors about this, I now know that I wasn't the only pastor stuck in that rut of measuring growth through church attendance. Every pastor fights the urge to count nickels and noses.

What if we shifted the focus from running out and grabbing as many people from outside of the community to bringing them in and spending more time discipling the people whom God has already entrusted to us? What if we decided to invest in those already attending week after week?

Immanuel Baptist Church in Morgan City, Louisiana — the first church I pastored — had a small congregation, about sixty-five people. These faithful few were passionate about the things of God and desired to grow in their faith. I chose a handful of men to invest in while my wife, Kandi, selected a few women with whom to do the same. It didn't take long for a discipleship initiative to spread through the congregation. Before leaving that

REDISCOVERING DISCIPLESHIP

church to pastor Brainerd Baptist Church three years later, God had grown the church numerically, but even more importantly, he had driven the roots of those relatively few members deep below the surface of a superficial Christianity. The seeds that were planted almost a decade ago are still being harvested today.

Believers who were at one time uncomfortable sharing their faith with lost friends before entering a discipling relationship were transformed into people living, breathing, and sharing the gospel. Their workplaces turned into a mission field for reaching the lost. Marriages were restored. Lives were changed. During the first year of ministry, we saw more people make decisions for Christ than were attending when I arrived. People regularly commented, "I feel like we are living the book of Acts." I felt the same way. By adopting a new scorecard for effectiveness in our church, the members followed suit.

Was it that we implemented something new? No. We rediscovered something old, as old as the church itself: discipleship. This rediscovery of discipleship has changed my own life as well. I often wonder how different my life would have been if certain men hadn't taken time to disciple me. But why stop with me? Let's take it a step further: How different would your life be today if you had an opportunity to be engaged in a Christlike, biblical discipleship relationship? How different would the lives around you be if you were the one to take seriously Jesus' command to make disciples?

K.I.S.S. Your Program Goodbye

A few years ago, our staff implemented a painful (though necessary) revision of our current programs. We applied something called the K.I.S.S. paradigm. Everyone on staff was encouraged to examine their ministries through the lens of our mission statement — Deliver, Disciple, Deploy — and to determine what things they needed to Keep, Increase, Start, or Stop (K.I.S.S.). Every ministry in our church was brought to the table. Nothing was off limits.

As Antoine de Saint-Exupéry once said, "Perfection is achieved, not when there is nothing more to add, but when there is nothing left to take away."[6] This kind of evaluation is very difficult because it removes what *you* want and reveals what *God* wants. Far too often we allow our egos to hinder spiritual growth in ourselves and those around us, when God wants us to toss aside our preconceptions, lay down what mankind sees as important, and embrace the mission to which he has called us.

In the movie *The Bridge on the River Kwai*, British prisoners of war in Burma during World War II are building a bridge for their Japanese captors. They devote enormous amounts of time constructing a bridge that serves as more than a channel for passage; it becomes something beautiful and wonderful for them. At the end of the film, there is a challenging moment when another group of Allied commandos force the captives to consider blowing up the bridge to keep Japanese trains from using it. It's a very difficult decision for the men because of the extraordinary effort they have expended in building the bridge. The men have become so focused on the intricacies of their effort that they have forgotten the larger mission of winning the war.

I share this because as you read this book, some of you may need to think seriously about eliminating some good programs in your church if you want to do what is best. Train yourself and your people not to be impressed with success in the church that does not accomplish the goal set forth by Christ: *making disciples*. Don't be impressed with momentary feats. Look for the fruit that lasts forever.

How many marriages were restored last year?

How many people are striving for holiness?

How many men and women are holding each other accountable?

How many addicts are experiencing victories over drugs, pornography, or alcohol?

How many groups are reproducing themselves exponentially?

How many fellow men and women are you investing in now?

In my first book, *Growing Up,* I wrote to those who wanted to be a disciple, those who longed to share in the heart of God. In it I introduced a system for spiritual growth that has been used in our own discipleship groups with great success. But in that book I was only able to scratch the surface of the what, why, and how of a discipleship group. In this book we will focus on the principal components of an effective D-Group, and I will show you how to implement that in your church.

So let's get started. The first step we must take is to repent. We must repent for being disobedient in the mission of the church — making disciples.

PART I

Know the Man Before You Go on the Mission

CHAPTER 1

The Master's Model
for Making Disciples

YOU WOULD LIKELY AGREE WITH me when I tell you that knowing *of* someone and *knowing* someone are two entirely different concepts. You may have heard of Winston Churchill, known as one of the greatest leaders of the twentieth century. He was resolute and immovable during a time when "the most powerful and influential men in Britain were determined not to offend Hitler"[1] by burying their heads in the sand and blindly following his lead. Yet despite his influence on the world, only a few people knew Churchill personally while he was alive. And among those few who personally knew him, only a handful could likely identify his place of birth, where he was raised, or what schools he attended.

I'm willing to bet you are unaware of the fact that Churchill plotted a map of the Middle East and established the country of Jordan.[2] Only a handful of people who lived at the time were privy to his personal life and were able to hear him speak about his personal pleasures, passions, or the principles that shaped his leadership style.

There is a difference between knowing *about* someone and *knowing* someone or something. I want to start by reminding you of this because in the midst of renewed attention on the topic of disciple-making there is also a significant level of confusion and noise. And before we talk about methods and strategies for discipling others, we need to get back to the basics. Knowing the term *discipleship* and understanding it in the way Jesus meant it are two different things. They can be chasms apart. Sadly today, some are throwing around the term *discipleship*, but they are speaking an entirely different language.

Before we dive into the principles and practices for obeying the Great Commission, we must learn to speak the same language. One of the most valuable principles I learned in studying herme-neutics — a theological term for the art and science of biblical interpretation — is that you cannot apply a text differently today from how it was applied in the context in which it was written. In other words, a text interpreted today cannot mean something entirely different from what it meant back then. Texts must be understood in their context. We can drift, albeit unintentional-ly at times, into heresy when we remove a text from its context. It might be helpful to remember it by this simple axiom: *a text without a context is a pretext for a proof text*. This applies to read-ing and studying a translation, but it also applies to Hebrew and Greek words, Hebraic concepts, and cultural practices.

Before we set out to obey Jesus' command to make disciples, journey with me back two thousand years to hear how he spoke the words of the Great Commission to the eleven men on the mountainside with him that day. The challenge in doing this is that we need to reprogram our Western ears to listen to that Galilean accent. Jesus was a Jewish man living in a Jewish land, observing Jewish customs and investing his life into Jewish men. Before we try to understand his message or mission, we must first learn to understand Jesus.

Know the Man

Jesus was a Jewish man, born to a Jewish mother, raised according to Jewish customs, speaking to a Jewish audience, and surrounded by Jewish disciples. The Bible is a Jewish book written by Jewish people, for a mostly Jewish audience, and is about a Jewish Savior who came to redeem both Jews and Gentiles. Don't misunder-stand me. I am not asking you to walk around with uncut corners of your hair, donning a yarmulke on your crown and frontlets on your forehead if you want to be a disciple of this Jewish rabbi.

Still, if you want to be a true disciple of Jesus, you must learn to know the Man. We must know the man before we can go on the mission to which we have been called.

Jesus was raised by exceptionally devout Jewish parents. They traveled to Jerusalem for Passover each year. He was circumcised on the eighth day of his life and was dedicated and given a Hebrew name. As he grew up, he regularly attended synagogue on the Sabbath, participated in every biblical Feast, studied and memorized the Scriptures, learned a trade from his father, and started his rabbinic ministry at age thirty — all of this according to Jewish customs at the time.

The fact that Jesus was a rabbi is validated by several places in the Bible where he is addressed this way. The word *rabbi* (pronounced like "Robby") literally means "my master." It was used to address a learned teacher or sage. A rabbi in Jesus' day was quite different from a modern-day rabbi. Jesus was an itinerant preacher, similar to a prophet of the Old Testament, and as such he either relied on the benevolence of others or had another occupation from which he derived his livelihood. In an age that lacked the highly developed, sophisticated methods of mass communication that we have today, a rabbi traveled from place to place to communicate his teachings and his interpretations of Scripture to the masses.

The late Rabbi Shmuel Safrai, a teacher at the Hebrew University, suggested that

> The traveling rabbi was the norm, rather than the exception. There were hundreds, perhaps thousands, of such rabbis circulating in the land of Israel in Jesus' day. These rabbis did not hesitate to travel to the smallest of the villages or the most remote parts of the land. They would often conduct their classes in the village or out under a tree.[3]

In some instances, classes would even be conducted in someone's home, similar to the small groups we have today.

According to the custom of the day, charging for teaching was frowned upon, so the itinerant rabbi was entirely dependent upon the hospitality and generosity of the community. Many rabbis carried their food with them — a pouch of meal and a few olives. This is how many of the teachers subsisted, not wanting to be a burden to their host. For the long-term Talmidim — those who were the rabbi's disciples — learning from a rabbi meant constant traveling, since the rabbi was always moving from place to place. If one wanted to learn from a rabbi, he had to "follow after him."

A rabbi was simply a teacher, and the term *rabbi* is interchangeable with the word we translate as "teacher" in the Gospels:

Luke 7:40: *Jesus replied to him, "Simon, I have something to say to you." "Teacher [Rabbi]," he said, "say it."*

Luke 10:25: *Just then an expert in the law stood up to test Him, saying, "Teacher [Rabbi], what must I do to inherit eternal life?"*

Luke 18:18: *A ruler asked Him, "Good Teacher [Rabbi], what must I do to inherit eternal life?"*

Matthew 22:23 – 24: *The same day some Sadducees, who say there is no resurrection, came up to Him and questioned Him: "Teacher [Rabbi], Moses said, if a man dies, having no children, his brother is to marry his wife and raise up offspring for his brother."*

Although he was clearly a rabbi, Jesus wasn't always referred to as rabbi. Like every other Jewish boy, he attended the religious academies at an early age to study the Torah. As a child, he grew "in wisdom and stature, and in favor with God and with people" (Luke 2:52). And as a humorous aside, I don't believe Jesus was one of those know-it-alls in the classroom. When his teacher asked, "Who can recite Deuteronomy 6?" he didn't respond, "I can. I wrote it." Jesus wasn't arrogant or condescending. Like any child, he grew and matured.

The Scriptures are silent about the time between Jesus' birth and a discussion he has at age twelve with teachers in the Jerusalem temple (Luke 2:41-50), but it's fair for us to wonder about his upbringing. Much debate has taken place about this time. What did he do? Where did he travel? Whom did he hang out with? What did he study?

We can fill in some of the blanks by assuming that Jesus was much like every other young boy in his culture at that time. As a Torah-observant Jew, Jesus would have learned the Hebrew alphabet as an infant. Parents were instructed in the Talmud, which is a commentary on the Scriptures by famous historical rabbis, to teach their children the alphabet — or "alephabet" — before they walked. Next, Jesus would have enrolled in the "house of instruction" or "school," the local synagogue. The first use of this word is found in Sirach (Ecclesiasticus) around 180 BC. Shortly thereafter, synagogues became the epicenter of learning, with the institution of the first district school system for youths being credited to the Pharisees around 75 BC.

Rabbis communicated to their young "Talmidim" — students — the importance of rehearsing older lessons. Knowing the old was just as important as learning new teaching. Professor Shmuel Safrai supports this pedagogical model for transformation:

> Individual and group study of the Bible, repetition of the passages, etc., were often done by chanting them aloud. There is the frequent expression "the chirping of children," which was heard by people passing close by a synagogue as the children were reciting a verse. Adults too, in individual and in group study, often read aloud; for it was frequently advised not to learn in a whisper, but aloud. This was the only way to overcome the danger of forgetting.[4]

Without notebooks to write in, computers to type on, or iPads to read from, first-century students relied on repetition and recitation for understanding. The Jewish Talmud, a commentary on the Old Testament Scriptures, cites the importance of reviewing: "He who studies the Torah and does not review is like one who plants and does not harvest."[5] Several other common sayings during this period give you the essence of the philosophy of teaching and training in Jesus' day:

"Your father brought you into this world, but your rabbi brings you into the life of the world to come!"

———

"If a man's father and his rabbi are both taken captive, a disciple should ransom his rabbi first."

———

"If his father and his master are carrying heavy burdens, he removes that of his master, and afterward removes that of his father."[6]

Clearly, Jewish culture at the time of Jesus placed a high priority on being a faithful student of the Scriptures.

Rabbinic Discipleship

You have heard the adage, "Knowledge is power." Historically, the Jewish people lived by this motto, with one caveat: the knowledge that leads to power must come from the sacred Scriptures. For this reason, the Jews have long been called a "people of the book." This was clearly evident in the way children and adults in that culture were taught — an approach that is drastically different from the educational system we have today.

There were several significant differences between the Jewish (Eastern) system of education and the Greek (Western) one. Norman Snaith summarizes some of these differences:

> The object and aim of the Hebrew system is *da'ath elohim* (knowledge of God). The object and aim of the Greek system is *gnothi seauton* (know thyself).... The Hebrew system starts with God. The only true wisdom is Knowledge of God. "The fear of God is the beginning of wisdom.".... The Greek system, on the contrary, starts from the knowledge of man, and seeks to rise to an understanding of the ways and nature of God through the knowledge of what is called "man's higher nature."[7]

These two systems are different all the way down to the roots.

Understanding these differences is important if we wish to understand how Jesus taught and what it means for us to call him our rabbi.

School Is in Session

Studying the Torah, according to the Jews, was the highest way of bringing glory to God. The *Mishnah* (or Oral Law) suggests, "If you have learned much, do not think highly of yourself for it, since for this you were created."[8] We continue to see the importance of regimented study today in the cultural values of orthodox Jews. Boys in Brooklyn, New York, begin studying the Torah at three years old. Steven Isaacs, in his book *Hasidim of Brooklyn*, writes,

> For an adolescent, the Torah is all. Six days a week, boys rise at 3 or 3:30 in the morning to go to the *mikveh* [ritual bath], are in school from 5:30 or 6 a.m. until nearly sundown, and then return to synagogue. After supper, they return to synagogue for the nightly study session. On Saturday, the Sabbath, they are in the synagogue all day.[9]

Josephus, the well-known Jewish historian, reveals that first-century Jews valued this as well: "Above all we pride ourselves on the education of our children."[10] Schooling consisted of three stages, each advancing in progressively more difficult increments. At the age of five, boys and girls would enter the *Bet Sefer* (the House of the Book), where reading and writing were taught using the Torah — the first five books of the Old Testament.[11] Next, students would graduate to the *Bet Talmud* (the House of Learning), where they would study the rest of the books of the Old Testament and a fragmented form of the oral law.

The brightest pupils then graduated to the *Bet Midrash* (the House of Study). The vast majority who didn't pass the entrance exam to this level of tutelage returned to their family business: carpenters, fishermen, or farmers. Before entering this doctoral level of education, would-be disciples (most of whom were fourteen to fifteen years old) were administered a series of tests given by the head rabbi on various topics such as the Torah, tradition, oral law, and customs. If the rabbi thought the student could make the cut, he extended an invitation to follow him until the age of thirty, which is when most rabbis began their own ministries. Three prominent first-century rabbis were Hillel, Shammai, and Gamaliel (who is mentioned in Acts 5:34).

Roy Blizzard and David Bivin, two authors in the emerging Hebraic Roots renewal movement, explain the uniqueness of a call from Jesus:

> When we see Him at the beginning of His ministry, He is walking along the shore of the Sea of Galilee and enlisting disciples with the call, "Come, follow me." "Follow me," LECH AHARAI (literally, "walk after me"), was a technical term in Hebrew for becoming a disciple. The call to discipleship sometimes necessitated heartrending decisions.... We recall the words of the man in Luke 9:61 who said to Jesus, "I will follow you, Lord, but first let me go say goodbye to my family."
>
> The call to discipleship often meant leaving mother, father, wife, children, relatives, friends and travelling the country under adverse and austere conditions. It meant leaving all. We can see this reflected over and over again in the Gospels. To the rich young man in Luke 18:22ff, the call to follow Jesus meant selling all that he had, giving it to the poor, and LECH AHARAI, "walk after me." Peter reminds Jesus (verse 28) that he and the other disciples are not like the rich man: "We have left 'ours' (i.e., home) and followed you." Jesus responded, "Amen, (You have, and that is commendable) I say to you, there is no one who has left house (i.e., home, family) ... for the sake of the kingdom of God who will not receive much more in this life, and in the age to come eternal life."[12]

The selection process was an intensive one, for sure. Knowing the cultural background of how a first-century rabbi selected his disciples gives us insight into the selection of Jesus' twelve disciples. Knowing this, the call of Jesus to "follow me" pops right off the page and strikes us in the deep places in our hearts, no matter how many times we've heard it before.

Most rabbis began their ministries at the age of thirty. They would eagerly wait for the brightest of pupils to approach them with applications to study, yet Jesus, a Nazarene who had earned the title "rabbi," wasn't waiting for people to come to him. He was out walking the shoreline and scoping out potential candidates. While most rabbis of the day would quiz prospective candidates, asking them top-of-the-class difficult questions about various laws and customs to find out if they truly had what it takes to continue with a formal Jewish education, Jesus was busy eyeing four fishermen coming in from a lackluster shift on the sea.

Fishing was a lucrative business in the first century, especially around the Sea of Galilee — but if you couldn't catch anything, you couldn't make any money. The fishermen we meet in the Gospels were struggling to fill their nets. They were former students who weren't good enough to be called to follow a rabbi after they had graduated from the *Bet Midrash*. To put it simply, they didn't make the cut in school, and they weren't making the cut at sea either.

Then one day there stood a rabbi before them — THE Rabbi — calling their names even though they didn't measure up. He invited them, young men who were, by themselves, not good enough by the standards of the world, and with these few he changed the course of history.

Jesus went against the typical pattern of his fellow rabbis by selecting his own disciples himself, rather than waiting for a line of would-be students to form. And this should remind us of an essential gospel truth — that we don't have to go looking for Jesus. He stands on the shore calling to us, waiting for us to answer his call and thus rescue us from our unworthiness. He is the first rabbi in history to go after his own followers. Aren't you glad he came looking for you?

Disciples Who Make Disciples

Jesus discipled the twelve men who would later change the world, and as he taught them, he gradually released them into ministry through a four-step process.

First, Jesus ministered, and the disciples watched him. In the Sermon on the Mount, Jesus taught God's truths while the disciples observed, listened, and learned as a part of the crowd (Matt. 5–7). When Jesus went into the synagogue and healed the lame, cleansed the lepers, and gave hearing to the deaf, the disciples were there to watch him (Mark 1).

Second, Jesus allowed the disciples to assist him in ministry. When Jesus fed the multitude, he broke the bread and performed the miracle, but the disciples distributed the supernatural meal to the hungry crowd and collected the surplus (John 6:1–13).

Third, the disciples did the ministry themselves, with Jesus' assistance. After his transfiguration, Jesus came down from the mountain and walked straight into a crowd in an uproar (Mark 9). The disciples had been trying to cast out a demon from a possessed boy, and they were failing miserably. In utter frustration and desperation, the boy's father turned to Jesus and asked him to intervene. "I brought my son to your disciples, but they could do nothing!" the despondent man cried (v. 17 paraphrased). Jesus stepped in, cast out the demon, and made the boy whole. Later, Jesus rebuked the disciples, who were powerless on their own, by saying, "This kind cannot be driven out by anything but prayer" (v. 29 ESV).

Finally, Jesus watched as the disciples ministered to others. Jesus sent them out with instructions to go into the world, cast out demons, and preach the gospel. And they came back saying, "Lord, even the demons are subject to us in your name!" (Luke 10:17).[13] Learning from a rabbi involved more than merely sitting in a classroom and listening to his words. As Ann Spangler and Lois Tverberg say,

> It involved a literal kind of following, in which disciples often traveled with, lived with, and imitated their rabbis, learning not only from what they said, but from what they did — from their reactions to everyday life as well as the manner in which they lived. The task of the disciple was to become as much like the rabbi as possible.[14]

Learning from a Master

Ange Sabin Peter, an accomplished potter, was given the privilege of studying for six months under Masaaki Shibata, an established Japanese potter. Spangler and Tverberg describe what a disciple relationship looks like by telling the story of Ange and master potter Masaaki Shibata in their book *Sitting at the Feet of Rabbi Jesus*. In this story, Ange was a potter who dreamed of studying under her hero, an old craftsman who was renowned for his brilliant pottery. Ange had studied pottery for years on her own wheel and finally got the chance to travel to Japan and learn under Shibata's teaching.

Since she wasn't from Japan, she was unaware of the Japanese tradition of being an *uchi deshi* that she was about to enter. An *uchi deshi* is an apprentice to someone who has perfected the art of pottery. According to the tradition, the *uchi deshi* — the student, generally a teenager — would not just attend lessons at the master's house, but would move in and be "adopted" into the family. Every part of their life would be lived alongside the master, for they had to learn to do *everything* the way that the master wanted it done. For this reason, *uchi deshis* would live for years with the master (with Shibata it was generally four), and only after many had passed would they be given the opportunity to throw the pots to which the master would feel worthy to inscribe his name.

However, Ange didn't feel as though she had the time for a four-year long apprenticeship. She figured that would be okay, since she had spent her own time learning how to throw pots on the wheel and assumed she wouldn't need as much time as a complete novice. She signed up for a six-month apprenticeship. Imagine her disappointment when she arrived at Shibata's door and was told to go work in the rice fields behind his house, then dig for clay the next day, and then wash dishes the next. "You cannot separate life from work," Shibata told Ange. "The way you do the most insignificant activity in your daily life will reflect in your work." During the entire six-month stay at Shibata's house, Ange did not fire one piece of pottery.[15]

In this case, the master's tutelage of his apprentice didn't merely consist of giving her a checklist of things to look out for while spinning the pottery wheel; it began by watching and waiting. Being a disciple of Jesus Christ is no different. Jesus will not simply train you to excel in one area or another. He begins with the relationship you have with him. Like the disciples he called on the seashore, no one warrants God's favor through meritorious works. It is through a grace-extended invitation from the greatest rabbi who ever lived.

The Bible reminds us that it's even worse, that we were at one time children of God's wrath (Eph. 2:3). We were enslaved by the patterns of the world and served the desires of our flesh, but "God, who is rich in mercy, because of His great love that He had for us, made us alive with the Messiah even though we were dead in trespasses. You are saved by grace!" (Eph. 2:4–5). The discipleship process always begins here, with a personal relationship with Jesus. Before we embark on a journey to learn how to invest in the lives of others, we need to come back to this. The first step in learning isn't gathering information about models and methods. Jesus doesn't start by changing our actions — what we do. He first changes our *heart*.

Network Marketing in Galilee

In the fall of 1995, my roommate Gino introduced me to a business opportunity that would change my life forever. Little did I know it at the time, but this venture would prepare me for ministry eight years later. The Public Business Reception, as it was called, was held at the Holiday Inn hotel every Thursday night in Metairie, Louisiana. At the first multi-level business meeting I attended, I was presented with a plan that promised me financial freedom in just a few short years. This was music to my ears! As a nineteen-year-old college student, I needed money. I had only one problem: coming up with the five hundred dollars required to sign up. So I presented my father with the rudimentary business proposal in the best sales presentation I could give. And I made him an offer: "If you provide the upfront cost and contacts, I will work the business until I can pay you back your initial investment." He agreed. The rest was history — or heartache, depending on whom you ask.

Within one week, my upline consultant, the one who signed me into the business, informed me that I had achieved Executive Field Trainer (EFT) in record time. I received this title by signing five people up in the business at five hundred dollars each. We were promoting local and long distance phone service as a product. Yet I soon learned that with new signees came new responsibilities as well. For the first time in my life, my success depended upon the success of those beneath me. I had to train, equip, and support the individuals in my down line. Within seven months, I had moved from EFT to Field Coordinator (FC). Each of my five signees replicated the process I had begun in them by enlisting five more people each to enroll in the business. The number of people working below me would determine how much money I would be making.

Obviously, this was a classic pyramid business, so it goes without saying that it didn't end well — but despite the conclusion of the story, I am convinced that many of the principles I put into practice to start a functioning business are sound. That business grew, not through advertisements or massive conferences, but by empowering a few individuals to replicate what I had done with them.

Some of these "network marketing" principles apply to the Christian life. First, success in a network marketing business is not measured by an individual's success, but on how well one empowers those beneath him. Zig Ziglar, my role model during those years of dabbling in a pyramid business, said, "You can have everything in life you want, if you will just help enough other people get what they want."[16] My success was dependent on the effectiveness of those below me in the organization. Applied to the task of making Christian disciples, we can say that the goal is not to execute everything you can by *yourself*; it's to invest in the people around you and to encourage them to do the same.

Second, Jesus understood better than anyone that replicating himself was the key to successfully expanding the scope of his ministry. In fact, he began a movement that is still replicating today! In John 14:12, Jesus explained to his disciples the extent of their ministry: "I assure you: The one who believes in Me will also do the works that I do. And he will do even greater works than these, because I am going to the Father."[HSCB] Some have wrongly interpreted this verse to mean that the disciples would do greater works in *significance* than Jesus. Yet this is clearly not the case, for nobody can do anything superior to what God has done.

What Jesus meant was that the *scope* of their ministries would be far-reaching. The works Jesus has in mind were of greater *quantity*, not *quality*. He was referring to the expansion of his ministry beyond the reach of one man, not doing works that would surpass the greatness of what God can do. While Jesus' ministry was essentially restricted to the regions of Judah and Galilee, those after him would go separate ways and proclaim the gospel to all nations of the world. Discipleship is a means to expanding the ministry of Jesus.

Third, every successful person in our business was required to formulate a game plan. Ignorance was certainly not bliss, and we wanted everyone to have a plan they could follow, a plan that would lead them to success. In addition, we initially required everyone to use the products before they sold them. You can't promote what you don't participate in. In the same way, *Jesus expects us to be a disciple before we can be a maker of disciples.*

The core to our business approach was inviting people to consider joining the business. Jesus told his disciples, "Follow me, and I will make you fishers of men" (Matt. 4:19 ESV). This is the essence of evangelism. It is never an end in itself — it is a means of recruiting followers who will in turn recruit others to be followers. In our business we empowered our new members to repeat the process that had been used to recruit them. Sound similar?

At some point, my network marketing illustration breaks down. While there are some methodological similarities, the goals are ultimately not compatible. For one, whether you were adopted in the family of God years ago or yesterday, we are all equal in the eyes of God because he loves us based upon the righteousness of Christ, not our good deeds or works. The foot of the cross is level ground for all. There are no levels of acceptance that we must work to earn from God. He is Father to all, and we are equally his children. Jesus' plan was to save the world from sin and restore us to God, not a get-rich-quick scheme to line the pockets of men.

How different would your life be if you lived with the goal of empowering others to succeed, even if they received all the accolades at the expense of our efforts? People want to know how much you care before they ever care how much you know. Before we examine the Master's model for making disciples, let's put on our Hebraic thinking caps and learn to see the world the way Jesus did.

CHAPTER 2

Think Like a Hebrew

"I HAVE HIDDEN YOUR WORD in my heart," writes King David, "that I might not sin against you" (Ps. 119:11 NIV). Have you ever stopped to think how strange this sounds? What does it mean to hide someone's words in your heart? Is David saying that his heart is like a box where he can store information? Of course not! He is using a metaphor that every Hebrew would have immediately understood.

A Hebrew would understand that the word "heart" refers to the mind, the center of being, the seat of intellectual thoughts, and "intestines" or "bowels" refers to emotions and passions.[1] Paul uses heart both ways. For example in Romans 1:21 and 10:6–9, "heart" is used to emphasize the mind, whereas in Romans 9:2 and Philippians 1:7, the emotions are being underscored combined with the thoughts of one's mind.[2] The apostle Paul, speaking to a Gentile audience in the book of Romans, said, "Do not be conformed to this world, but be transformed by the renewal of your mind, that by testing you may discern what is the will of God, what is good and acceptable and perfect" (Rom. 12:2 ESV). If his audience were Jewish believers, Paul may have inserted the word *heart* for *mind*.

As we began to see in the last chapter, if we want to journey with Rabbi Jesus, we must learn to stop thinking Hellenistically and start thinking Hebraically. I'll admit that this is easier said than done. Brian Knowles writes,

> We [Western thinkers] ... insist on rendering everything into logically consistent patterns, on systematizing it, on organizing

it into tight, carefully reasoned theologies. We cannot live with inconsistency or contradiction. We feel compelled to think antithetically. The Godhead must be tightly defined and structured. We cannot live with the Hebraic idea that God is simply ineffable, and that God's Book doesn't lend itself to systematization.[3]

But how have we abandoned our Hebraic roots? Where did we first diverge from an Eastern thought process? It's popular to say that Hebrews think with two hands. This means learning to balance seemingly contradictory ideas. For example, on one hand we have the idea that God selected his chosen people before he created the world. On the other hand, there is the idea that we must choose him. Or consider prayer. God knows what we are going to say before we ask, but still he commands us to pray.

The Hebraic way of thinking is more comfortable holding these concepts in tension because Jews tend to prefer word pictures, stories, poetry, imagery, and symbolism to the "Western" or "Greek" preference for words, ideas, definitions, outlines, lists, and bullet points. The goal is not simply to resolve a problem or arrive at a conclusion. When a rabbi tells a story, he speaks to the heart first and the head second. Traditionally, Western ways of thinking tend to speak to the head first and the heart second. Since the majority of the Bible was written by Hebrews to Hebrews, those who read it from a Westerner's frame of mind tend to overlook many of the nuggets of wisdom buried throughout.

To this point, we have been speaking in generalities. So let's explore the disconnect a bit further by asking a simple question. If you were to go to an American seminary and ask the students there a simple question: "What is God?" what would you hear as an answer? My guess is that you would hear statements like, "God is righteous; God is holy; God is love; God is wise." You would certainly hear several references to the "omni's": omnipotent, omnipresent, and omniscient.

If, on the other hand, you were to go to a Yeshiva, an Orthodox Jewish school for learning in Jerusalem, the students there would answer that same question quite differently. "God is a rock," they'd say. "God is living water. God is an eagle's wings. God is fresh-baked bread."

Close your eyes and think about the words you hear in each setting. At the seminary: love, holy, wise, omnipotent, omnipresent, and omniscient. What do you picture? If you're like me, your mind's eye pictures words or letters. Now picture the responses from the Yeshiva: living water, a rock, an eagle's wing, and fresh-baked bread. What do you see? Or maybe a better question is, What do you feel? If you linger long enough, you may be able to smell the bread coming from that hot stone oven. Hebraic culture radiates emotion, and so does the language.

The Word Is the Foundation

The Hebrew Bible, what we refer to as the Old Testament, is composed of three sections, collectively referred to as the *TaNaK*. Each of the consonants in this word represents one of the three sections. (The **a**'s are supplied for context.) The Jewish Bible contains the same books as our modern Old Testament with one exception — the order is different.

The **T** stands for the Torah, the Law. The **N** stands for the Nevi'im, the prophets. (The Hebrew word for "prophet" is *nevi*.) Finally, the **K** is for the Ketuv'im, or the writings, which contains most of the wisdom literature and poetic books of the Old Testament.[4]

- Torah (Law, Teaching): Genesis, Exodus, Leviticus, Numbers, and Deuteronomy.
- Nevi'im (Prophets): Joshua, Judges, Samuel, Kings, Isaiah, Jeremiah, Ezekiel, Hosea, Joel, Amos, Obadiah, Jonah, Micah, Nahum, Habakkuk, Zephaniah, Haggai, Zechariah, and Malachi.
- Ketuv'im (Writings): Psalms, Proverbs, Job, Song of Solomon, Ruth, Lamentations, Ecclesiastes, Esther, Daniel, Ezra, Nehemiah, and Chronicles.

Hebrews placed enormous significance on learning and understanding the Torah, or the Law. When Jesus rebuked the leadership of Israel, he said to them, "Woe to you, scribes and Pharisees, hypocrites! You pay a tenth of mint, dill, and cumin, yet you have neglected the more important matters of the law — justice, mercy, and faith" (Matt. 23:23). The Law was sacred to the Jewish people, a source of delight and joy for people who lived to please their God. But many Jews got stuck in a legalistic approach, a system of rules, rather than seeking the goal of the law — a transformed life under the rule of God.

Within the Torah, God reminds the people to hold fast to the Law of God, to keep it central in their life and worship. Jewish historian Shmuel Safrai writes,

> Torah study was a remarkable feature in Jewish life at the time of the Second Temple and during the period following it. It was not restricted to the formal setting of schools and synagogue, nor to sages only, but became an integral part of ordinary Jewish life. The Torah was studied at all possible times, even if only a little at a time.... The sound of Torah learning issuing from houses at night was a common phenomenon. When people assembled for a joyous occasion such as a circumcision or a wedding, a group might withdraw to engage in study of the Law.[5]

The apostle Paul explains the significance of the Torah in Romans: "So then, the law is holy, and the commandment is holy and just and good" (Rom. 7:12).

Interestingly, the first books of each of the latter sections (Nevi'im and Ketuv'im) both begin with a commendation to obey God's Law. The first book of the second section, the Nevi'im, is Joshua. After Moses passed the baton to his lieutenant, Joshua, God outlined for Joshua a prescription for success: "Above all, be strong and very courageous to carefully observe the whole instruction My servant Moses commanded you. Do not turn from it to the right or the left, so that you will have success wherever you go" (Josh. 1:7). The phrase "the whole instruction" refers to the teaching of God in the Torah.

In effect, God is saying, "Do you want to be effective as a leader, Joshua? Do you want to be successful in your life and ministry? Then follow the law." Notice what the Lord says next: "This book of instruction must not depart from your mouth; you are to recite it day and night so that you may carefully observe everything written in it. For then you will prosper and succeed in whatever you do" (v. 8). If Joshua is to be successful, he must meditate on and memorize the law.

In the first book of the Ketuv'im (the Writings), the Law of God is once again stressed as essential to fruitful living before God. Psalm 1 starts out by pronouncing a blessing on the man who will set his heart on the Law. The psalm then contrasts this with the wicked man who does not delight in the Law, even foreseeing the futility of those who dismiss God's instruction.

Two Paths to Follow

Let's put on our Hebraic glasses for a moment and visualize the truth conveyed in Psalm 1. The English Standard Version sketches the first verses for us clearly:

> Blessed is the man who walks not in the counsel of the wicked, nor stands in the way of sinners, nor sits in the seat of scoffers; but his delight is in the law of the LORD, and on his law he meditates day and night (vv. 1–2 ESV).

As we have seen, Hebrew language communicates with word pictures. Here the psalmist begins by conjuring up some very specific images for the people who would be singing or listening to this psalm. The goal is to show them a downward progression, to highlight the person we are not to be. Notice the three different verbs in the first half of the verse: walk, stand, sit. You can picture it this way:

When you follow the advice of the wicked, you stop walking.

When you take the path of sinners, you move from standing to squatting.

When you squat, you're frozen. Your growth is at a standstill. Your devotional life is nonexistent, and your affection for the Lord is cold.

But there is an alternative path as well, which is pictured in verse 2. It says that the other man's delight is in the Lord's instruction, and he meditates on it day and night. What is the easiest way to avoid the trap of a downward-spiraling sinful lifestyle? To delight in the Law and to meditate on it.

Two Outcomes for Our Choices

The psalm continues with vivid images:

> He is like a tree planted beside streams of water that bears its fruit in season and whose leaf does not wither. Whatever he does prospers. The wicked are not like this; instead, they are like chaff that the wind blows away. Therefore the wicked will not survive the judgment, and sinners will not be in the community of the righteous" (vv. 3–5).

This visual imagery highlights two distinct outcomes to the paths that we take, both of which are connected to our faithfulness to the Word.

The first outcome is pictured as a fruitful tree planted by streams of water. This is a tree that has been purposely planted by someone. It has been picked up and placed in fertile ground, firmly planted to withstand whatever storms may come its way. That's what God does for the man or woman who meditates and obeys the word of God. The land might be dry and barren. The air might be hot and humid. But if the tree is planted by the streams, so that it can sink its roots down and draw nourishment, it will be prosperous.

On the other hand, those who are influenced by the world and others are like dry chaff: the loose hulls that are separated from grain by threshing or rubbing the wheat between one's hands. There is no stability for chaff, no security except for the knowledge that it will be blown clear of the grain when wind comes.

Those who are like chaff will be driven and tossed by the waves and wind of their environments. They are unstable and unsure.

Picture What I'm Saying

As already mentioned, Hebrew is a language emanating emotion, rather than one for calculated certainties. Hebrews think in pictures; Westerners think in bullet points and lists. If you were to close your eyes and think about the terms *wise, love, righteous,* or *holy,* what comes to mind? For me, words appear. Perhaps definitions.

Jesus, as a Jewish rabbi, taught in pictures. Bread was a concept that Jesus continually connected to Himself. Bread, or manna, was the source of sustenance during the Exodus from Egypt to the Promised Land. Jesus used the same imagery when tempted by Satan in the desert. "Man must not live on bread alone, but on every word that comes from the mouth of God" (Matt. 4:4). Jesus' first response to the devil connected bread to the Scriptures.

Even the city into which Jesus was born spoke of bread. Bethlehem is made up of two Hebrew words: *bet* and *lechem. Bet* is the Hebrew word for house, and *lechem* is the word for bread. Jesus was born in the house of bread or a bread factory.

After providing bread for the people after their departure from Egypt, God instructed Aaron to store manna in the Ark of the Covenant as a reminder of His provision in Exodus 16:33: "And Moses said to Aaron, 'Take a jar, and put an omer of manna in it, and place it before the LORD to be kept throughout your generations" (ESV). The contents of the Ark of the Covenant are explained in Hebrews 9:3–4:

> Behind the second curtain, the tabernacle was called the most holy place. It contained the gold altar of incense and the ark of the covenant, covered with gold on all sides, in which there was a gold jar containing the manna, Aaron's staff that budded, and the tablets of the covenant.

Bread was a symbol of spiritual sustenance coming from heaven, a foreshadowing of Jesus. The city Jesus was born in spoke of bread. Micah 5:2 records,

"But you, O Bethlehem Ephrathah, who are too little to be among the clans of Judah, from you shall come forth for me one who is to be ruler in Israel, whose coming forth is from of old, from ancient days" (ESV).

Bread for Life

Jesus executed two different feeding miracles, both involving bread, in two different locations. This carries a special weight that would have been heavy in the minds of the Hebrews. The twelve tribes of Israel inhabited the western region of Palestine, the region that became known as the Land of the Twelve. According to Jewish tradition, the Decapolis, or "Ten Cities," was known as the Land of the Seven. Ray Vander Laan suggested on his site Follow the Rabbi that the Land of the Seven was named so because it represented

> the seven pagan nations driven from Israel in Joshua's day. Jews believed that the area was dominated by the devil. The pagans were known for worship of fertility gods, and many of their practices were detestable to God's people.[6]

Keep this thought in mind as we examine the two feeding miracles. After the multiplication of bread in the feeding of the 5,000 — with women and children, there were probably more like 15,000, even 20,000 people — Jesus enlisted the disciples with a task: gather the leftover bread in baskets. Isn't this odd? Why didn't he send the leftover bread home with the people? Couldn't he have left the pieces for the wild dogs that roamed the land? Jesus is about to teach an unexpected lesson with bread.

Upon completion of the task, the disciples likely lined up before Jesus. He counted out loud, "1, 2, 3, 4, 5, 6, 7, 8, 9, 10, 11, and 12." Each of the disciples held a basket in hand. Jesus was visually demonstrating that he was the bread of life for the twelve tribes of Israel. The food was multiplied for more than merely feeding one's stomach; he showed them that he was their source and sustainer and that he was capable of providing for every need.

The disciples were slow learners, however. They missed the meaning of the miracle. Mark 6:51–52 says, "And he [Jesus] got into the boat with them, and the wind ceased. And they were utterly astounded, for they did not understand about the loaves, but their hearts were hardened" (ESV). A few chapters later, Jesus gave them a second chance at the mid-term exam.

The disciples were following their Master through the region "of Sidon to the Sea of Galilee, through the region of the Decapolis" (Mark 7:31). Remember that the Decapolis was considered the land of the Seven.

A crowd gathers. Jesus performs yet another feeding miracle, and then he sends his disciples out again to gather up the leftovers. However, this time, Mark 8:8 records the exact number of baskets that were filled with leftover bread: "Then they collected seven large baskets of leftover pieces." He counted out loud again, "1, 2, 3, 4, 5, 6, and 7."

Unbelievably, the disciples, much like us, are slow to understand, forcing Jesus to connect the dots for them. Mark 8:17–20 reads,

> Aware of this, [Jesus] said to them, "Why are you discussing that you do not have any bread? Don't you understand or comprehend? Is your heart hardened? Do you have eyes, and not see, and do you have ears, and not hear? And do you not remember? When I broke the five loaves for the 5,000, how many baskets full of pieces of bread did you collect?"
>
> "Twelve," they told Him.
>
> "When I broke the seven loaves for the 4,000, how many large baskets full of pieces of bread did you collect?"
>
> "Seven," they said.

Without saying a word, Jesus communicates, "I am not only the God of the Jews, but I've also come to save pagan Gentiles." This concept was not in their paradigm. Even though God said to Abraham that the nation of Israel would be a light to the nations, they believed he would redeem only them. Jesus destroyed their model by blowing their minds. We can read these stories and miss it because we aren't thinking Hebraically!

Jesus plainly explained in John 6:35: "I am the bread of life. No one who comes to Me will ever be hungry, and no one who believes in Me will ever be thirsty again." His ministry culminates at the Last Supper when he palms a thin slice of bread. He holds it up and basically says, "This is my body. The bread that will sustain you will be broken. And after it's broken, it will feed everyone who believes. Take it, and eat it." Everything they have been taught up to this point about manna was a foreshadowing of the Messiah.

Did He want us to eat His flesh? Of course He didn't. He completes the thought: "Do this in remembrance of me" (Luke 22:19). He commanded them to accept him, his teachings, his life, and his example. He urged them to remember his words, obey his truths, and savor his teaching. He asked his disciples not to live on bread alone, but "on every word that comes from the mouth of God." And he communicated this all by breaking a piece of bread, a foreshadowing of his sacrifice to come on the cross.

I know what some are thinking at this point: "Why didn't Jesus just come out and *say* all of that stuff? Why didn't he simply state, 'I am the God of Israel, but I'm *also* the God of the Gentiles'? Why was he so cryptic about something so important?" But see, he *did* come out and say it — except as a Hebrew, not as a Westerner.[7] He painted a picture instead of listing a sheet of facts, and pictures are worth thousands of words. Jesus' lordship isn't something to memorize, like information for a test; it is Truth to embrace. The Rabbi didn't fill the mind with endless bullet points of the goodness of God; he wanted you to taste, see, and experience that the Lord is good.

Hellenism Infiltrates the World

In order for those of us who live in Western culture today to understand much of the Hebraic mindset, we must exert considerable effort to learn about the original culture and the context in which Jesus lived and taught. Christianity was once almost entirely a Jewish religious movement. The people to whom our

Bible was written back then would have understood these images without any trouble. So what happened to change that? How did we lose these Eastern ways of thinking?

To understand what happened, we must go back in time to Alexander the Great, the sharpest military leader ever to walk the planet (with the exception of Maximus). A few centuries before Christ, Alexander conquered almost all of the known world with his military strength, cleverness, and diplomacy. He did it so well that it spawned some of the most spectacular war myths known to mankind. As legend would have it, Alexander and a small company of soldiers approached a strongly defended, walled city. Alexander, standing outside the walls, raised his voice and demanded to see the king. The king approached the battlements above the invading army and agreed to hear Alexander's demands.

"Surrender to me immediately," commanded Alexander.

The king laughed. "Why should I surrender to you? We have you far outnumbered. You are no threat to us!"

Alexander was ready to answer the challenge. "Allow me to demonstrate why you should surrender," he replied. Alexander ordered his troops to line up single file and begin marching. He marched them straight toward a sheer cliff that dropped hundreds of feet to the rocks below.

The king and his soldiers watched in shocked disbelief as, one by one, Alexander's soldiers marched, without hesitation, right off of the cliff to their deaths. After ten soldiers had died, Alexander ordered the rest of his men to stop and return to his side.[8]

The king and his soldiers surrendered on the spot to Alexander the Great, though not because of the size of his army. You see, when the Persians or the Babylonians would conquer a region, they would immediately overturn the society through sheer force. Victims would be presented with two options: bend the knee to the empire or suffer persecution, imprisonment, or death. Rome did the same thing years later.

But Alexander sought to control those he defeated in an entirely different way. Bypassing the use of muscle, he would seek to bend the will of the people he was conquering. He infected his would-be converts through manipulation. Conquered communities were not stripped of their nationalities or cultures. Rather, he offered them a self-serve buffet in *addition* to their traditions. No one was forced, under the rule of Alexander the Great, to follow a particular path over another. Instead, he presented them many options from which to choose.

Beginning with Alexander's rule over Judea in 330 BC, the Greeks began exporting their cultural values to the people of Israel through what is now referred to as Hellenism. Alexander and later rulers were so successful in doing this that by the time of Jesus three hundred years later, Greek was the common tongue of the Mediterranean world. The New Testament was written in Greek. Alexander accomplished this cultural transformation by focusing on four areas: entertainment, athletics, information, and education.

Alexander set up educational centers to teach world religions, Greek mythology, world history, astronomy, mathematics, philosophy, and anything else that can be taught. Suddenly, the Jews who received all of their lessons from the sacred texts of the Tanak were being given all kinds of extra-scriptural information. The Greeks didn't prohibit Torah learning, however. In fact, they encouraged it! Yet they tried to add to it by encouraging teaching about their own gods and goddesses as well.

Alexander erected libraries next to synagogues containing Hellenistic writings and a system to teach Greek values and ideals. In essence, he said, "Keep learning what you're used to learning, but don't stop there! Come learn from us. Don't be closed-minded. We'll enlarge your minds and expand your horizons!" His tactics were so subtle that most Jews didn't realize that they had been infected until it was too late.

The second way Alexander introduced Greek culture to the Jewish people was through athletics. Greeks invented competitive sports as we know them today. The predecessor to our present-day Olympic Games was the Isthmus Games. Since those games were held at Corinth, the people to whom Paul wrote would have understood one of his chief metaphors for the Christian life: "Don't you know that the runners in a stadium all race, but only one receives the prize? Run in such a way to win the prize" (1 Cor. 9:24). Paul was picking up on a common image at the time to explain the type of commitment required by a follower of Christ.

This type of athletic competition was largely foreign to the Jews. You will never get your hands on a Jewish Book of World Records, because it doesn't exist. "Why would I want to compete against my brother?" they would ask. "He labors alongside of me for the same cause against the same enemy." Yet when Alexander introduced the games, they grew to be quite popular. Even the levitical priests were drawn to the Decapolis to watch the men compete naked. As a result, the daily duties of the priesthood were hindered because there just weren't enough priests willing to work in the temple. Greek culture had captured the imagination of the Jewish people.

The third thing that Alexander did was to set up an outpost for the dissemination of information. He brought in art, music, and news from all around the world. Prior to his influence, Jews cared little about the world at large. Soon, however, they were exposed to the "Greek Weekly" and the "Roman Times Free Press." Rugs, furs, and commodities were imported from around the world. Pottery and furnishings were sold and traded in Greek-controlled stations throughout the land. Was there something wrong with this? In itself, no. But these changes led to a subtle influx of new ideas and exposed God's people to other cultures that drew the people's focus from the things of God to the things of the world.

The final method that Alexander implemented in his Hellenization program was the erection of theaters for performances. The Greeks invented tragedy and comedy plays as we know them today. In fact, the layouts of our modern theaters are based on those of the ancient Greeks. Even the word *hypocrite*, as used by Jesus in Matthew 6, is a Greek word used to describe the masks that actors and actresses used during a play. (A hypocrite is some-one who pretends to be someone they are not.)

Again, these things are not bad, necessarily — but with each progressive step, the tolerance of God's people was lowered. Their standards for righteousness changed as they sought to make these new cultural influences compatible with their Jewish culture and belief system. And this kind of cultural influence is still happening today! Some worship sports teams at the expense of God. Their lives are ruled by athletics, whether in the form of travel ball, high school football games, or rigorous collegiate training schedules. Nighttime television is littered with choice words and sexual innuendos. PG–13 movies used to be suitable for thirteen-year-olds, but no longer. News outlets have hijacked the dissemination of information and spin an event into an oppor-tunity to push an agenda.

Discerning truths from lies is increasingly difficult. Our kids are being taught that the world began, not with the bang of God's Word, but by the grandest display of cosmic happenstance ever conceived. They are learning that nothing is absolute, so "live and let live" is the best way to coexist. Biblical accounts have been reduced to children's stories.

What is my point? Simply that while there are great cultural differences in understanding the Hebraic mindset, many of the challenges we face are similar to the challenges faced by every first-century Jewish man or woman. Every culture is in the pro-cess of sliding away from the truth of God, and this means that it is increasingly important to immerse ourselves in the Word of God, to be formed and shaped by what God says, not by the val-ues and words of our culture. But this is not something we can do by ourselves. In this book we will see how to keep close to the heart of Christ, and in chapter 13 you will learn an extremely practical method for judging its effectiveness.

Right now, you just need to make a decision. You need to de-cide which of the people in Psalm 1 you wish to be. Will you be the chaff, freshly threshed and carried away by the wind, or will you be the tree uprooted from your inhospitable soil and placed next to the streams by the Gardener? Will you be tossed away from the useful grain, or will your roots stretch deep and wide so that the fruit of your branches will bloom?

CHAPTER 3

A Picture Is Worth a Thousand Words

REMEMBER THE FIRST TIME YOU watched a sporting event or a movie on an HD television set? The players looked three dimensional, as if they were in the living room with you. Movies mimicked your memory: vivid and full of detail. The action was intense, the fight scenes thrilling, and the romance emotional. The same movie or sporting event you had seen perhaps many times before came to life from a different point of view.

As we began to see in the first two chapters, the Bible is filled with Hebraic insights that we miss when we read it for head knowledge only, or worse, as a checklist of tasks to accomplish. Each account in the Bible was written as something to be meditated over. Smells, sights, and sounds are meant to be savored. Can you come to saving faith in Jesus Christ without understanding these insights? Of course you can. But a disciple should be motivated to know what his Master knows, to learn and digest everything his Master has to teach. Placing ourselves in the Hebraic context of the first century brings many of the biblical accounts into high definition.

Surfing the Internet in Israel

Naturally, the Internet was nonexistent in the first century, but the concept of Scripture-surfing — the idea that you could move from one idea or reference in Scripture to another one — was quite common. I was first introduced to this idea by the late Dwight Pryor, founder of Judaic Christian Studies, when I met him at a Haverim school in Dayton, Ohio. The subject of the four-day retreat I was attending was "The Messiah and the Apostle," in which we were comparing Jesus' theology in the Gospels to Paul's theology in the Epistles.

My roommate for the week was a Jewish rabbi who believed in Yeshua (the Hebrew way of saying Jesus' name) as his Messiah. He had studied under Dwight before and his understanding and knowledge of the Old Testament Scriptures were like nothing I had encountered. As you can imagine, I was overjoyed by my room assignment. For the next three days, my gracious roommate entertained hundreds of questions from a young, eager-to-learn seminary student.

The first night, as we were talking and getting to know each other, he caught me off guard with a question: "How do you share the gospel with a lost person?" I rattled off a few chapters and verses from the Romans Road, a presentation that would have earned me an iron-on patch in AWANA. When I turned the question back around to him, his answer was quite different. He said to me, "I start with the fall in Genesis and continue through the Old Testament."

"Really?" I asked.

"Of course!" he replied. "We both have the same goal. To communicate the gospel. The only difference is our starting point. You begin in the New Testament with Paul's epistles. I share the gospel the way Jesus would have, beginning with Genesis."

Stunned, I turned the lights off and marinated on his words all night.

My interest was piqued. Over the next few days, I learned how to identify what Pryor, our instructor, called *keshers*. These were references in the New Testament that point readers back to particular verses and chapters from the Old Testament. Not having studied the Old Testament in any depth, I wasn't able to do this very well — at first.

Let me give you an example of what a kesher looks like. Have you ever noticed how when Jesus mentioned a word or phrase, his audience seemed to instinctively know what he was talking about? Unlike most western Christians, Jews committed the Scriptures to memory at an early age and could recall them without much effort. Keshers are connections or linkages that a rabbi would make in his teaching, connecting it back to the Old Testament. These connections are sprinkled all throughout the New Testament. Think of them as hyperlinks on a webpage — hover over a link and your arrow turns into a hand. As soon as you click on the link, you are instantly transported to a different page.

Every culture has something similar. If I said to you, "'Twas the night before Christmas," what would you say? You might follow my words by saying, "And all through the house, not a creature was stirring, not even a mouse." The first line of the poem brings to mind the rest of the poem. It's an allusion that you recognize.

Or take the phrase "Our Father, who art in heaven." You would probably respond, "Hallowed be thy name." Finally, how would you respond if I recited the words, "Amazing grace, how sweet the sound"? Without missing a beat, you would sing back, "That saved a wretch like me." Connecting what you were teaching or saying to something in the Scriptures was a common way of communicating, and it was a method used by the early Christians as well. That's why our Bible is filled with keshers. Let's look at a few.

Linking Back to the Old Testament

Before accepting the challenge to approach Pharaoh about letting God's people go, Moses inquired of God, "If I go to the Israelites and say to them: The God of your fathers has sent me to you, and they ask me, 'What is His name?' what should I tell them?" (Ex. 3:13). God told Moses to say, "I AM WHO I AM. Tell them that I AM sent you" (v. 14 paraphrased). This passage was commonly known because it was the revelation of God's name: I Am, which is a form of the verb in Hebrew that means "to be." While it can have many meanings, it essentially means that God is the God of yesterday, today, and forever to come.

Now consider what Jesus says in John 8:58. A Jewish ear would immediately make a linkage to the self-disclosure of God's name when Jesus said, "Before Abraham was, I am." We might ask today, "Why didn't Jesus just say that he was God instead of beating around the bush?" But you'd be missing the point. Jesus *did* just say that he was God. He said it as a Jew, not an American.

Or consider another example. After calling Zacchaeus, a Jewish tax-collector, down from the tree, inviting himself over to his house, and sharing a meal together — a practice that was despised by the corrupt, religious leaders of his day — Jesus said, "Today salvation has come to this house" (Luke 19:9). As I mentioned above, the Hebrew way of saying Jesus' name is Yeshua, which is translated as "salvation." In saying this, Jesus meant that salvation had come in two ways. In one way it came to Zacchaeus's house to have dinner, since Jesus' name means salvation. Yet, in another sense Jesus had come into Zacchaeus's heart to dwell. Jesus closes this conversation with these words: "Because he too is a son of Abraham. For the Son of Man has come to seek and to save the lost" (Luke 19:9–10). Salvation had come, both physically and spiritually, to the "house" of Zacchaeus.

Additionally, it helps if we understand that the phrase the "son of man" refers to a messianic title used in Daniel 7:13 about the coming of the Lord. Also, the phrase "seek and save the lost" is a concept discussed in Ezekiel 34 where God comes to gather up His lost sheep. Jesus draws upon both of these Old Testament passages to say that salvation has come fully in him, his presence and his power (cf. Ezek. 34:11, 12, 16, 23).

The Kesher on the Mount

One of my favorite keshers is found in the dialogue between the Father and the Son on the Mount of Transfiguration (Matthew 17).

Many significant events happen on mountains in the Bible. In the life of Jesus we find him preaching on a mountain in Mark 3, praying on a mountain in Mark 6, and being tempted on a mountain in Matthew 4. Jesus taught the Sermon on the Mount, even though it was probably a plain, in Matthew 5 through 7, and he issued the Great Commission on a mountain in Matthew 28.

Jesus uses mountaintop excursions as teachable moments for his core group of disciples (Peter, James, and John).

In Matthew 17 we read that while he was praying on the mountaintop, Jesus' face shone white. This kesher points the reader to Moses' encounter with God on the mountain in Exodus 34:29. As Jesus' face is shining, the disciples who were with him noticed two unexpected guests: Moses and Elijah. The presence of Moses and Elijah on this mountain is another reference — one that, when understood, is simply astounding.

First of all, students of the Hebrew Bible (the Old Testament) would have been aware of many similarities between Moses and Elijah. Both men met God personally on a mountain (Ex. 33:18–23; 1 Kings 19:9–18). Both witnessed God displaying his glory. Both had memorable departures. Moses was buried by God himself on Mount Nebo; Elijah was whisked away in a chariot of fire. Moses founded Israel's economy; Elijah restored it. Both men also had a symbolic presence in traditional Jewish culture: Moses represented the Law, and Elijah represented the prophets. In that moment, standing with Moses and Elijah, Jesus was quite literally glorified in the midst of the Law and the Prophets.

"While he was still speaking," the text continues, "suddenly a bright cloud covered them, and a voice from the cloud said: 'This is my beloved Son. I take delight in Him. Listen to Him!' When the disciples heard it, they fell facedown and were terrified" (Matt. 17:5–6). The cloud in this text is another kesher, a direct reference to Moses' experience on Mount Sinai in Exodus 24:15–16. If you recall, Moses went up to a mountain enveloped in clouds to witness the manifest presence of God.

The high point of the transfiguration of Jesus, however, was more than a glowing face and a cloud. It was the moment when God spoke audibly: "This is my Son!" These words should sound familiar! They were the same words spoken to Jesus at his baptism: "You are My beloved Son; I take delight in You!" (Mark 1:11) One difference here is that, while the words at the baptism were directed toward the Son as a confirmation of his divinity

(*You* are my Son), the words on the mountain are directed toward the disciples (*This* is my Son).

To fully grasp the significance of the words spoken on the mountain, I want you to feel the weight of what God says here: "This is my beloved Son. I take delight in Him. Listen to Him!'"

- **"This is my beloved Son"** is a quotation from the Ketuv'im (the Writings) in Psalm 2:7. "I will declare the LORD's decree," writes the psalmist. "He said to me, '*You are my Son*; today I have become Your Father.'" Psalm 2 is often labeled a "Messianic Psalm," speaking of the coming Messiah. Coincidence? I don't think so.

- **"I take delight in Him"** is from the Nevi'im (the Prophets). It is a direct quote from Isaiah 42:1: "This is My Servant; I strengthen Him, this is My Chosen One; *I delight in Him.*" This entire chapter in Isaiah, like Psalm 2, points to the Messiah — it speaks of his mission.

- **"Listen to Him"** comes from the Torah (the Law) and is a kesher from Deuteronomy 18:15: "The LORD your God will raise up for you a prophet like me from among your own brothers. You must *listen to him.*"

Up until this point in the life of Jesus, the disciples had misunderstood Jesus' true identity. Thus far, the only ones to accurately confirm and affirm who Jesus is are the demons (Mark 5:7). Dwight Pryor sums up the full weight of these links to the Old Testament:

> God Himself answers Jesus' question by linking together three Messianic Scriptures from each of the three sections of the Hebrew Bible: the Torah (Law), the Nevi'im (Prophets), and the Ketuv'im (Writings). God is saying, by using these three short sentences, "Jesus is my Son, the promised Messiah of Israel foretold by the prophets of Old, and He is the fulfillment of every section of Scripture. He is the embodiment of My Word; He is Word-made-flesh. Listen to Him! Obey Him!"[1]

The disciples should have understood this when Jesus affirmed that he had not come "to destroy the Law or the Prophets. I did not come to destroy but to fulfill" (Matt. 5:17), but they didn't — they needed it to be spelled out for them by God. On the mountain, the dots were connected for Peter, James, and John — connecting Jesus to Moses and Elijah, to the promises of the Old Testament. The Mount of Transfiguration, as well as the entirety of Jesus' ministry, was a testament to who he was.

Does It Really Matter?

We see in the ministry of Jesus the fulfillment of the Old Testament Scriptures. God gave the seven feasts of Israel to Moses; Jesus fulfilled every one of them with his coming. Jesus died on Passover, was buried on the day of the Feast of Unleavened Bread, was raised on the day of First Fruits, and descended from heaven in the power of the Holy Spirit on Pentecost. His life, death, and resurrection parallel the feasts and festivals of Israel.

After leading the Israelites out of Egypt on Passover, Moses traveled around for fifty days before ascending Mount Sinai for an encounter with the Living God. From the day of Passover, Jews would count the *omers* (days) until Pentecost — much the way our children do leading up to Christmas — in order to give thanksgiving to God for the grain harvest. According to the sages of Israel, God descended on Mount Sinai in the desert to give Moses the Law on the first Pentecost before speaking God's word to the people below (Ex. 19–20).[2]

After Jesus' death, burial, and resurrection, he appeared to his disciples and others for forty days (Acts 1:3), and then ten days after that, the Spirit descended on the disciples during Pentecost. In the same way that Moses waited for fifty days for the manifest presence of God to be poured out on Mount Sinai, the disciples waited fifty days to be filled with God's Spirit on Pentecost. Peter, undoubtedly aware of this connection, begins to preach the Word of God to the festival attendees.

Luke records that 3,000 people were saved after Peter's Pentecost sermon. Now that we're accustomed to looking for keshers in the Bible, we can better understand why the number 3,000 is significant. The answer can be found in Exodus 32. Just after Moses descends from the mountain from his communion with God, he finds the people he's been leading through the desert worshiping a calf made from melted golden trinkets. When he is questioned, his brother Aaron justifies the actions he and the people have taken by saying, "It just popped out the fire by itself." (I don't know about you, but I've yet to see flying golden calf figurines emerge from a bonfire.) God was not pleased.

Moses declared,

> "This is what the LORD, the God of Israel, says, 'Every man fasten his sword to his side; go back and forth through the camp from entrance to entrance, and each of you kill his brother, his friend, and his neighbor'" (Ex. 32:27).

The number of people that died that day was 3,000.

Is it a coincidence that Acts 2 reports that 3,000 were saved at Pentecost? Hardly. Thousands of years before, those who were led by the light plunged themselves into darkness, and 3,000 people died because of it. Then in Acts 2, God pulls back the veil of reality and reveals the redemption possible through his Spirit by descending upon the people who have ascended the Temple Mount. This mirror-image of the mountaintop experience at Sinai led to the birth of the church, and 3,000 people were snatched from the clutches of Satan that day.

Why is this important? Because it reminds us that the Bible is an inexhaustible book, one in which we must continually immerse ourselves. It is the primary means by which we come to know God. You cannot know the God of the Word unless you know the Word of God. In order to understand God, you must know Jesus — the walking Word (John 1:1, 14) — which is impossible apart from the Scriptures. The disciples didn't understand who Jesus was at first because they overlooked the blatant signs staring them in the face. They had the Scriptures, but didn't understand them. I'm afraid that we, as a modern audience, are strapped into similar sandals.

On Looking Ahead

In addition to the way we approach the Scriptures as a modern, Western audience, we also have different understandings of certain key biblical concepts. Consider the idea of *eternal life*, for instance. Western understandings are often influenced by medieval paintings, or we picture a celestial paradise where we spend forever with God in heaven, both of which are true. But biblically, eternal life begins when life here on earth is over. Conversely, for the Hebrew, the kingdom of God begins in this life, and our existence after death is merely a continuation of what has begun here. Eternal life is life that is harmonious with God in the world that he created. This is one reason why Jews greet one another with "shalom," or peace.

Now, if a man walked up to the majority of Christians today and asked, "What do I need to do to inherit eternal life?" what would their response be? They might respond as I did to my Jewish roommate by walking the person through the Romans Road. Or maybe they would explain the ABCs of salvation: Admit, Believe, and Confess. They might encourage the hearer to repeat a prayer asking Jesus to be the Lord of their life. At one time or another, I have utilized every one of these practices.

But when a man came up to Jesus and asked, "Teacher [Rabbi], what good must I do to have eternal life?" the response was quite different. Jesus responded to his question with a question of his own: "Why do you ask Me about what is good?" Then Jesus continued, "There is only One who is good. If you want to enter into life, keep the commandments" (Matt. 19:16–17). Is Jesus suggesting that salvation is by works? No. He is saying that to experience the power and the presence of God we must live in obedience to his commands. The kingdom of God is not just an invisible place in a spiritual realm; it is a movement among God's people in the here and now. You don't need to wait for the kingdom of heaven to arrive. It's already here, in part, and will fully come when the King returns.

In a helpful series entitled *The Kingdom of God*, Dwight Pryor describes the kingdom using three different concepts. He talks about the kingdom as a *person* who is the fulfillment of all of Scripture — Jesus (Col. 1:19). The kingdom is also a *power*; as Jesus said, "The kingdom of God has come near you" (Luke 10:9). And the kingdom is a *place*; God has "seated us with him in the heavenly places in Christ Jesus" (Eph. 2:6 ESV). If we want to be disciples, those who live under the rule of the King, we need to know him personally, live in his power, and look forward to the day when the kingdom of God on earth is as it is in heaven. How do we become the kind of people who are fit for the kingdom? By knowing and obeying the Word of God.

Unity in the Community

Hebraic and Western mindsets also differ in one other way. They tend to see the relationship between the *community* and the *individual* in very different ways. Westerners will speak about having a personal relationship with God. Jews, however, typically did not speak of salvation as an individual experience; for them, it is corporate. And this carries over into the New Testament church. When Jesus teaches his disciples to pray, he doesn't begin with "*My* father, who art in heaven." He says, "*Our* Father." Communal living was an essential component of spiritual development. Growth was not something that happened in isolation and seclusion.

Jewish life revolved around the community, and the community shaped the rhythms of the day, the week, the months, and the years. The Jews lived together, ate together, traveled together, prayed together, and stayed together. When Jesus was left behind in the temple after a festival visit to the city, it wasn't all that unusual. His parents probably assumed he was traveling with his relatives. The community was an extended family, and people watched out for one another, providing for needs and taking care of each other.

Comfort in the Question

As a young believer attending seminary, I was honored and privileged to be discipled by a man named David Platt. David is the author of a best-selling book titled *Radical*, and he has a genuine passion for discipleship. When I first began meeting with David for discipleship, however, he employed a particularly frustrating technique with me. Whenever I would ask him a question, he would respond with a question. At first, I thought he was being evasive, but I soon learned that he was being intentional in doing this. He had learned this approach by studying Jesus.

So if I were to ask him, "What do you think about speaking in tongues?" he would reply by asking me, "What do you think?"

"David, can a person lose their salvation?"

"What do you think?"

"How can I know that I'm saved?"

"What do you think?"

"How does one know that he is saved?"

"What do you think?"

Maddening. But intentional and calculated.

As we saw earlier, Jesus often answered questions with further questions. He didn't do this to avoid the question or to be a jerk; it was a way that he, as a trained rabbi, could better gauge the understanding and intention of his audience. Questions engage hearers in something akin to a tennis match, with each participant proving their understanding by keeping the ball in play through each ensuing question. The sage lobbed the first question. The student would internalize it, formulate an answer, and share it in the form of another question. This practice requires a deep grasp of not just the question asked, but the answer and its implications. If you were to ask a rabbi why he answers a question with a question, he is likely to answer you by asking, "Why not?"[3]

Jesus *constantly* answered questions with questions. If you want to take a deeper look at this, you can start with several passages in Luke's gospel: Luke 11:14ff.; 12:41ff.; 18:18ff.; 24:13ff. Understanding that this was a teaching technique is helpful. It reminds us that the purpose of a rabbi was to raise up Talmidim (disciples), who would not only know what the rabbi knew, but would become who the rabbi was. In Pirke Avot 1:1, the first line of the Mishnah, or Jewish commentary on the Scriptures, it says, "Moses received Torah from Sinai and Joshua to elders and elders to Prophets and men of the Great Synagogue." Discipleship was something that was culturally embedded into the DNA of the Jewish people. Disciples lived, ate, traveled, listened, and studied under their rabbi. A good disciple, as one rabbi put it, was "covered in the dust of their Rabbi."[4]

We no longer live in a culture where discipleship is essential to our learning, growth, and maturity. So how can we experience it as a follower of Jesus Christ? Is it still possible to be covered in the dust of the Great Rabbi? Absolutely! And we can begin by looking at the men whom Jesus called to follow him. Hopefully, by my exposing you to the idea that Jesus is a Jewish rabbi, you will be inspired to dig deeper in the Scriptures, to better know the man you want to be like, to understand how he lived, what he taught, and how he made disciples. The Bible is like a multi-cut diamond. The more you gaze into it, the brighter it shines.

CHAPTER 4

Disciple-Makers Are Made, Not Born

WITH THE ADVENT OF COMPUTERS, many of us today spend time sitting — more than ever before. And that isn't always good for your health. Studies have shown that being sedentary throughout the day, day after day, week after week, can actually take years off your lifespan. Our bodies need to move, they need some form of exercise and activity each day.

One of the simplest ways to get that is by walking. Walking is undeniably good for the body. The simple act of moving your legs and arms simultaneously and elevating your heart rate benefits you socially, emotionally, and physically. Walking relieves stress, boosts your mood, enhances sleep quality, strengthens the heart, provides energy, and promotes overall health. It's mentioned frequently in the Bible as well, though not for the healthy benefits. Walking is good for an additional reason — it leads to maturity.

Before the invention of the automobile, people walked more often than they do today, which is why it is used so often as a metaphor in the Bible. Hippocrates may have been the one to say, "Walking is man's best medicine," but it is God who emphasizes, "Walking is man's best way to maturity." In the Bible, the Christian life is portrayed as a walk. God walked with Adam in the Garden. "Enoch walked with God; then he was not there because God took him" (Gen. 5:24). God instructed Abraham to go on a long walk on faith, which he obeyed. And even more miraculous, Abraham somehow convinced his wife to go with him, even though they had no idea where they were going! Can you picture what that must have been like?

"Abraham, where are we going?"

"Ur … Ur … Ur … I don't know. God will reveal it to us when we get there."

Or consider how God enlisted Moses to lead his people out of Egypt toward the Promised Land. What was supposed to be a six-month journey turned into a forty-year excursion, during which God led in a pillar of flame by night and a cloud of smoke by day. And notice the instruction God offered to Joshua as the Israelites were entering the land of Canaan:

> "Moses My servant is dead. Now you and all the people prepare to cross over the Jordan to the land I am giving the Israelites. I have given you *every place where the sole of your foot treads* [wherever you walk], just as I promised Moses" (Josh. 1:2–3, emphasis mine).

The theme of walking with God continues into the New Testament as well. Jesus began his earthly ministry by inviting Peter, Andrew, James, and John to "come follow me," or literally, "come *walk* after me." For the remainder of their lives, they followed his lead, even to their death. Every disciple of Jesus is walking somewhere and following someone. So, who are you following? Where are you headed?

Come Walk with Me

As morning broke, the first light of day spilling out upon the Sea of Galilee, the glow revealed several hardworking men tending their nets after a long night of fishing. As fishers on the lake, they worked during the cool nights when the fish were feeding. In the morning they would push through their exhaustion in order to clean the fish, mend their nets, and sell the catch to the markets and townspeople. Several hours of work awaited them each night, so they were off to catch a few hours of sleep for their weary bodies. First-century fishing was an arduous job.

On this particular morning, as the fishermen were coming in from another long night, they encountered a Nazarene rabbi who extended an invitation to them. Although it was a simple offer, they knew that it was a truly life-changing opportunity. How they chose to respond would forever change their lives and the lives of the human race as we know it.

Mark 1:16–20 recounts the call of these young men. It's our introduction to them:

> Passing alongside the Sea of Galilee, he saw Simon and Andrew the brother of Simon casting a net into the sea, for they were fishermen. And Jesus said to them, "Follow me, and I will make you become fishers of men." And immediately they left their nets and followed him. And going on a little farther, he saw James the son of Zebedee and John his brother, who were in their boat mending the nets. And immediately he called them, and they left their father Zebedee in the boat with the hired servants and followed him (ESV).

The Participants

Peter, Andrew, James, and John were fishermen. Fishing was their occupation. You may enjoy fishing on calm afternoons or in the mornings on vacation, but these men were professionals who worked the night shift. Every day they let down their nets, caught fish, cleaned fish, sold fish, and slept to fish again tomorrow. Day after day they repeated this.

Peter, like many of us, had a foot-shaped mouth. He spoke before he thought and was always ready for a confrontation at a moment's notice. Yet, over time Jesus rounded off Peter's jagged edges and honed his charismatic personality from a hot-tempered fisherman to a compassionate shepherd of God's flock. On the day of Pentecost, this fisherman delivered one of the clearest presentations of the gospel in human history, resulting in the salvation of 3,000 people.

Andrew, Peter's brother, was also an evangelist, someone who constantly brought people to Jesus. He understood not only who Jesus was, but what he was here to do. Andrew is remembered as the disciple who spotted the young boy with the lunch that Jesus used to multiply the fish and the bread in John 6. Andrew had eyes for others, seeing immediately how God might use them for his kingdom purposes.

James, the son of Zebedee, was the first of the original twelve to die as a martyr. His zeal for Christ would cost him his life. During Jesus' earthly ministry, he, along with Peter and his brother John, were invited to be a part of Jesus' D-Group, a small group of four who met with Jesus for private instruction.

John, James' brother, is called the disciple whom Jesus loved. John went on to write more books of the New Testament than any of the other Twelve. For John, Jesus pulled back the veil of reality and allowed him to peer into the future after being banished to the Isle of Patmos. John's writings are recorded in a gospel, several letters, and what we know today as the book of Revelation.

The fact that these men were fishermen was not by happenstance; it was by God's design. And at the very least, it should tell us that if God can use these ordinary men, he can use anyone. Each of these men began their discipleship journey without much, at least by the world's standards. Let's look at some of the things that characterized them.

1. The disciples were blue-collar workers

As already mentioned, Peter, Andrew, James, and John were fishermen. Simon the Zealot was a card-carrying political activist, and Matthew was a government employee. Each understood the importance of hard work.

2. The disciples possessed no formal religious training

In chapter 1 we postulated that these men didn't make the cut coming out of school. In fact, what most amazed the religious leaders at the time was the fact that the apostles had such power and authority without having been formally trained in their schools of theology. Acts 4:13 records the response of these religious leaders: "Now when they saw the boldness of Peter and John, and perceived that they were uneducated, common men, they were astonished. And they recognized that they had been with Jesus" (ESV). An intimate relationship with Jesus is more significant than any achievement garnered or degree earned.

3. They were young men

In 2006, I attended a conference taught by Ray VanderLaan, the founder of *Follow the Rabbi Ministries*. Ray first exposed me to the startling notion that the disciples were most likely young men, ranging in age between 13 and 20 at the time of their calling. Peter was likely the oldest. We know that Peter was married, because his mother-in-law is mentioned in Mark 1:30. Also, Peter was often the spokesperson — albeit self-appointed at times — for the rest of the disciples, and he appears to have had governance over his boat. All of this signifies that he's something of an accomplished seaman and not a novice. As for the others, are you not convinced about their young age? Well, here are seven reasons why the disciples may have been young adults at the time of Jesus' invitation.

———

Title — Jesus chose two terms to describe His disciples: *Mikronos*, which means "little ones," in Matthew 10:42, and *Teknion*, which means "little children," in John 13:33 (KJV, ESV). In both cases, the terms are synonymous with the word "disciple."

Training — Although I mentioned this process earlier, it's worth repeating. In the Mishnah Avot 5, a Jewish commentary on the Old Testament, the ancient Jewish pedagogical system is explained as follows:

Scripture study begins at age 5;

Mishnah study at 10;

Torah obligations at 13;

Continued rabbinical study at 15 if chosen to be tutored by a formal teacher;

Marriage at 18;

Formal teaching at 30.[1]

Formalized education was completed by age 15 unless one sought out the tutelage of a rabbi. These small few who were chosen by a rabbi were afforded an opportunity to study under a teacher until the age of 30. This means that the overwhelming majority of students entered the workforce, many times continuing the family business. Since the disciples were already working, we can assume they were disregarded for formal education by the rabbis when Jesus called them.

Traveling — A teenager is more likely to engage in continuing education, since a man over 30 leaving his trade would have been countercultural and shunned. Most disciples began traveling with a rabbi at the age of 15 or 16. We know that the disciples had left their jobs and families behind. After a difficult teaching, Peter said to Jesus,

"Look, we have left everything and followed You."

Jesus replied,

"I assure you,… there is no one who has left house, brothers or sisters, mother or father, children, or fields because of Me and the gospel, who will not receive 100 times more, now at this time — houses, brothers and sisters, mothers and children, and fields, with persecutions — and eternal life in the age to come. But many who are first will be last, and the last first" (Mark 10:28–31).

It's apparent that the disciples had left behind their old life, both spiritually and physically. We have no reason to believe Jesus' disciples were the exception to the acceptable norm of working a steady job.

Marital Status — It was the custom for a Jewish boy's marriage to be arranged by his parents before the age of 18. Peter is the only disciple we know of who was married. We can speculate that the other disciples were too young to be married, since bachelors in the Jewish culture were frowned upon. Personally, I believe the leaders of Israel would have added this aberration to the list of already mentioned attacks against Jesus and his disciples if it were the case.

Temple Tax — According to Exodus 30:13–14, the temple tax was required at Passover from every male aged 20 and over. We have record of only two of the men in question paying the temple tax: Peter and Jesus. Jesus instructs Peter in Matthew 17:27 to "go to the sea and cast a hook and take the first fish that comes up, and when you open its mouth you will find a shekel. Take that and give it to them for me and for yourself" (ESV). Although we can't be certain, we can speculate that the other disciples were underage and therefore exempt from paying the tax.

Longevity — Early Christian traditions concerning the apostles may support the idea of younger men. Due to the length of their ministries after Jesus' death and the late dating of the Johannine and Petrine letters, one can assume the disciples were young adults when Jesus summoned them to follow him.

Immaturity — The disciples exemplified behavior characteristic of younger men. Whether it was their arguing over who is the greatest, unawareness that a devil was living among them for three years, their inability to grasp theological truths, or their fearfulness on two occasions of torrential downpours on the Sea of Galilee, all signs point to the likelihood that they were in the teen years. Furthermore, most mothers don't speak up for their adult sons about seating assignments at the marriage supper as James and John's mother did one day (Matt. 20:20ff.). Taking into account their youth, it helps us to make sense of why Jesus had to teach them again and again. They may not have lacked intelligence — they may have just been immature.

———

At the end of the day, it's hard to know for certain if the disciples were teenagers. In an email poll conducted by a pastor, several New Testament scholars agreed with the idea that they were young men.[2] Even assuming that this is true, we must also be careful that our lack of understanding about the life of an adolescent in the first century does not warp our perspective.

We need to realize that Jewish boys become men at thirteen after their bar mitzvah celebration. The word "bar" means "son of," and "mitzvah" is the word for commandments. So a thirteen-year-old

Jewish male, living in the first century, would have already assumed responsibility for his own life by shouldering the commandments of God. In essence, he has entered the process of maturity. As Paul said to the Corinthian church, "When I was a child, I spoke like a child, I thought like a child, I reasoned like a child. When I became a man, I put aside childish things" (1 Cor. 13:11). A "teenager" of the first century would be nothing like a teenager living today. We still consider young teens to be children in our culture.

At the same time, it is worth challenging our cultural norms here. Perhaps we should consider entrusting younger men and women with ministerial duties. Some of the ripest believers for discipleship may be younger adults who are in this stage of life: moldable, shapeable, flexible, and available with a future discipleship ministry of many years still ahead of them.

Why have we spent so much time looking at the ages of the disciples of Jesus? I believe that one of the greatest disservices we have done to the apostles through the ages has been to glamorize them. Don't get me wrong! They are men we should respect and even revere for their faithfulness to God, but at the end of the day they were no different from you or me. These were ordinary, hardworking men who answered an invitation from a Galilean rabbi, an invitation that would lead to their changing the world.

Jesus bypassed the theological institutions of Jerusalem, the wealthy cities of Jericho and Sidon, the intellectual sects of the Pharisees, Sadducees, and Scribes, and called these twelve ordinary men to follow him. Aren't you glad he still extends the same invitation to ordinary, average men and women today?

A Disciple Follows Christ

So what does it look like to follow Jesus? When a student followed a rabbi, his allegiance was to the Torah, not to the rabbi. The student followed the rabbi to learn the Scriptures, first and foremost.

Notice, however, what Jesus does *not* say when he calls his disciples. He doesn't say to them, "Hey, I want you guys to come learn systematic theology with me. Let's discuss theories of creation and the fall! Let us examine ethical manners of living and working with others." No. He simply said, "Follow me!" This call was personal. It was something more than a call to study; it was a call to a person. He invited the disciples into a distinct relationship with him. Author Bill Hull highlights the need to be Jesus-focused in our discipleship:

> I am to live as though Jesus is living in me. If Jesus were a plumber, what kind of plumber would He be? If He were an attorney, what kind of attorney would He be? If He were an accountant, teacher, business owner, what kind of person would He be?[3]

Discipleship has an end goal: to be conformed into the image of Christ — to talk the way he talked, walk the way he walked, and respond the way he responded. It begins with an unshakeable allegiance to Jesus, which is why I believe that only a believer can be discipled (see chapter 10). Of course, that doesn't mean we don't study or share Scripture with an unbeliever. We just need to call it evangelism!

Don't forget that the call from the Master is just that — a call. Jesus comes looking for us. The disciples did not have to seek him out; he found them. And this is still how Jesus does it. In fact, we are incapable of looking for him apart from his grace. We are dead in our trespasses and sins, sinners enamored with our sin and blinded by the god of this world from seeing the light of the gospel, the glory of Christ (Eph. 2:1–3; 2 Cor. 4:4).

To make disciples effectively, we must first recognize that a disciple is one who is pursued by Christ, has been found and called by him, and has made the decision to follow him. As a disciple-maker, all you're doing is pointing at the One you're following and saying to those around you, "Come with me; I'm following him."

A Disciple Is Formed by Christ

Jesus, the author and perfecter of our faith, is the one who forms and makes disciples. When he first called his disciples, he said to them, "Follow me, and I will make you become fishers of men" (Mark 1:17 ESV).

The word "become" here is related to the word for "make." One lexicon says that it means "to experience a change in nature and so indicate entry into a new condition."[4] It connotes the idea of something coming into existence through maturation.

"Becoming" is a long process that Jesus brings about in our lives over time. It's not an instantaneous gift, but the result of an extended, intimate relationship that develops over time. Jesus is the originator of the action. We cannot grow in him on our own, but we *can* align ourselves with him, so that he may grow us. We can put ourselves in a position to experience the abundant, victorious life that God has envisioned for us. This is the essence of what we refer to as "discipleship."

My book *Growing Up: How to Be a Disciple Who Makes Disciples* provides a roadmap for growing closer to Christ. The first three chapters build a case for making disciples. The fourth chapter describes a process for growing in godliness that is based on 1 Timothy 4. The remaining chapters unpack an acronym, CLOSER:

- **Communicate** with God through prayer,
- **Learn** to understand and apply God's Word to your life,
- **Obey** God's commands,
- **Store** God's Word in your heart,
- **Evangelize** (share Christ with others), and
- **Renew** yourself spiritually every day.

Regularly practicing even one of these disciplines will increase your spiritual fervor. And the more of them you cultivate in your life, the closer you will grow to the Lord, becoming like Christ. Incorporating them into a weekly discipleship group (the D-Group) will change your life.

Before pastoring my first church, it's fair to say, I knew nothing about growing vegetables. But two of the members of my church, Mr. Jimmy and Brother Ed, soon made sure that I knew what I was doing in the garden. They arrived at my house one morning with a truck full of dirt, tillers, shovels, stakes, and plants. Working together, we shoveled the grass away, tilled the ground, put the black gold topsoil down. (I didn't know what it was made of, but it sure didn't smell good!) We planted tomato bushes, peppers, cucumbers, and okra.

But that was just the beginning. After they left, the real work began. Every day, I watered. Every few days, I pulled weeds. And I waited. I watered some more, spread fertilizer, and waited. I watered some more and then, just for good measure, waited. I would go out every day to check the plants, only to be disheartened when nothing seemed to be growing. Then, one day, something changed. Overnight, several of the plants shot out of the ground and began growing. The work we had done had prepared the soil, fashioning a fertile environment for the vegetables to take root. But there was nothing I could do to actually make the plants grow. That was God's work. We plant, we water, we wait — but it is God who brings the increase (1 Corinthians 3:6).

Your life is similar to my experience as a gardener. By yourself, you are incapable of producing spiritual fruit, but you *can* plant yourself in a position to experience it. That's the value of being in a group where you are intentionally pursuing Christ with other believers, what I'm calling a D-Group. Discipleship is more than a weekly group gathering, but never less.

A Disciple Is Focused on Others

Jesus enlisted his disciples into service by giving them a mission. To accentuate what he *did* say, let's first look at what he *didn't* say:

"Follow me, and I will make you holy,

Wise,

Happy,

Prosperous,

Smart, or

Successful!"

Instead of telling them what they might gain for themselves, Jesus focused their attention outward. When he called his disciples, he immediately let them know that they would be molded into a Delta Force army that would reach people with a message of redemption and hope. They would be fishers of men.

Some have reduced this command to soul-winning or sharing one's faith, but the scope of the agreement transcends simple evangelism.[5] Jesus elaborates the mission further in Matthew 28:19: "Go, therefore, and make disciples of all nations." This is more than a call to evangelize. Evangelism is embedded within the discipleship process. We will take a closer look in chapter 10 at the relationship between evangelism and discipleship and explore their interconnectedness.

Fishing, not catching

Did you happen to pick up on what the brothers were doing when Jesus first approached them? They were casting their nets and mending their nets. Mark 1:16–19 reads,

> Passing alongside the Sea of Galilee, he saw Simon and Andrew the brother of Simon *casting* a net into the sea, for they were fishermen. And Jesus said to them, "Follow me, and I will make you become fishers of men." And immediately they left their nets and followed him. And going on a little farther, he saw James the son of Zebedee and John his brother, who were in their boat *mending* the nets (ESV, emphasis mine).

When I studied martial arts, I learned that anything can be used as a weapon, whether it be a tree limb, a broom handle, or the stapler off a desk. In the same sense, Jesus uses whatever is at hand as a teaching tool to develop and disciple. *Life becomes the classroom for discipleship, and class is always in session.* Jesus used the fishermen's occupation to teach them; the tools of their trade were transformed into tools for teaching the things of God.

In Jesus' day, fishermen cast their nets repeatedly into the water to catch fish. They tossed a circular net measuring about twenty feet in diameter, weighted down by heavy bars of metal or rocks attached to the edges. Tossing it away in a circular motion, the goal was to land it like a parachute in the water. As the net descended to the bottom of the lake, the fish swimming below it would be trapped in the netting. The fishermen would then dive out of the boat, swim to the bottom, gather the weights, and drag the entire net back to the boat or onto the shore.

As you can imagine, this process was laborious and repetitive, and there were no guarantees that they would catch anything. But that didn't diminish the importance of casting the net. The only way to catch fish was to continually cast the net, throwing it out again and again, time after time. Sometimes the net would be full. At other times it would be empty. But that's the nature of fishing. You cast, and the rest is up to God and the fish.

Ministry with Jesus is exactly the same way. He has called us to cast the net, but he's responsible for the catch. We cast; he catches.

Fixing the nets

After a long night of fishing, James and John were busy in the boat with their father, engaged in the loathsome practice of repairing their nets. A torn net was as useless to a fisherman as a boat without a sail is to a sailor. The word for "fix" or "mend" is rendered in several different forms in its nineteen occurrences in the New Testament. It can mean to prepare, restore, create, complete, or unite. There are two nuances to the meaning of the word that I want to identify here that apply to our study of discipleship.

The first is similar to the way the word is used by the apostle Paul in 2 Timothy 3:16–17: "All Scripture is inspired by God and is profitable for teaching, for rebuking, for correcting, for training in righteousness, so that the man of God may be complete, *equipped* for every good work." This is similar to the word *mending* or *repairing* and can mean "to put in appropriate condition, or to furnish or fit completely."[6] This sheds light as to why the translators chose to use the words "complete" and "equipped." The same word is also found in Ephesians 4:11–12: "He gave the apostles, the prophets, the evangelists, the shepherds and teachers, to *equip* [or mend] the saints for the work of ministry" (ESV, emphasis mine).

In other words, even though these would-be disciples thought they would be catching fish and mending nets for the rest of their earthly lives, God had a different plan for them. He was preparing them for their future profession of *casting* for the lost and *equipping* the saints. And even if you are not a fisherman, I can assure you that he's been doing the same in your life as well! God has been preparing you for ministry through every setback and success you have had. Jesus knows your past, and he knows your future, and he doesn't waste an experience.

From the very beginning, starting with his initial call, Jesus implanted the seed of multiplication within the hearts of his disciples. Jesus didn't call them to come, sit on a pew, and listen to a pastor preach. His call was to fish, to cast for others. Jesus had it in his heart for you to go out and make disciples among the nations. Do you see the difference? It's a focus outward, toward others. It's another reminder that the Christian life is not about you or me. *The gospel has come to us because it is heading to someone else.* We are just another link in the chain, and each of us is either fumbling the handoff or passing the baton.

A Disciple Forsakes Everything

When Jesus extended the invitation to his disciples to follow him, they responded — without hesitating. They *immediately* dropped what they were doing and followed him. In this we learn that obedience precedes service.

Joey Bonifacio, author of *The Lego Principle*, once began a message by asking a group of pastors to associate a product with a particular brand. "I'm going to say a brand or a popular trademark," he told them. "I want you to answer, in only one word, the business the company represents. Let's start here: 'Starbucks.'"

The room answered, "Coffee."

"Toyota." "Cars."

"Rolex." "Watches."

With each brand, the attendees chimed in without hesitating, until he got to the final one.

"The Church."

At that, the room fell silent. The pastors were thinking, trying to come up with a word that would describe the "business" of the church. What's that "one word?"[7] What would your answer be?

I know what my word would be: Discipleship.

One of the greatest problems we face in the church today is that we have outsourced the task of disciple-makers and have depended on a handful of "full-time" ministers to do the job that Jesus gave to us. We will never carry out the Great Commission if only full-time vocational ministers are making disciples. Discipleship wasn't *a* ministry of the first-century church. It was *the* ministry of the church.

Shouldn't it be ours as well?

CHAPTER 5

A Forgotten Practice

OVER THE YEARS, OUR UNDERSTANDING of discipleship has changed — and not always in a good direction. Discipleship has shifted — from an ongoing process over the course of one's life to a class you sign up for and complete.

When older members of my denomination, the Southern Baptists, hear the word *discipleship*, it brings back memories of the "training union" of the late 1960s. These were set up because "the normal Baptist formation tools were finding it difficult to succeed," comments Molly T. Marshall. "Sunday School, Training Union, and the missionary organizations were all scrambling for their existence and seeking new ways of forming disciples."[1] The shortcomings they experienced led to several new approaches, and two new organizations emerged from this movement: the Navigators and Campus Crusade for Christ.

Campus Crusade was founded by Bill Bright as a ministry to reach the lost through evangelistic events. His desire was to begin discipling those who responded to an evangelistic appeal to follow Christ. Campus Crusade may have been the first organization to do this in the United States, beginning in 1947, and some of its early success can be attributed to partnerships with scholar Daniel Fuller and evangelist Billy Graham.[2] The ministry was known as an

> aggressively evangelistic movement, which places a strong, wholesome emphasis on the living Christ, the authority of the Scriptures, the importance of the Church, personal and group evangelism, the ministry of the Holy Spirit, and the adventure of Christian discipleship.[3]

In 1976 Bright wrote the foreword to a foundational work on discipleship entitled A *Guidebook to Discipleship* and included these words on the purpose of his organization:

> Campus Crusade for Christ International believes that the awakening of the first century will be duplicated in our time through the Church, the Body of Christ, under the direction and control of the Holy Spirit, as Christians win people to Christ, build them in the faith, and send them out into a ministry of discipleship. Though our ministry is best known as a ministry that emphasizes evangelism, far more emphasis is placed on discipleship.[4]

Bright did not see his work as something entirely new; rather, it was his goal to emphasize Jesus' model for making disciples.

I believe Bright was correct — the work of making disciples is nothing new. In fact, as we have seen, it is an ancient practice, one that Jesus developed and used for his own purposes with his own disciples and one that continued in the early church. During the first couple of centuries, various forms of discipleship continued that followed the Jewish tradition. Yet as time passed, the original understanding of what it means to make disciples was lost as new cultural understandings replaced the context of the early Christian church and those first believers.

In this chapter I want to introduce you to several key leaders from the past two thousand years of church history, figures who in various ways were used by God to preserve and recover elements of a biblical understanding of discipleship. As we learn from these leaders, my hope is that we can begin to rediscover a fresh vision of discipleship for our churches today.

We begin in the fourth century with one of the most notable figures in Christian history — the bishop of Hippo in North Africa, Augustine.

Confessions of a Disciple-Maker

Theologian, church father, apologist, and preacher are words that may be used to describe the ministry of Augustine. However, disciple-maker is a descriptor not often associated with debatably the most influential theologian of Northern Africa.

For many years Augustine wasn't influencing the world for Christ, but rather was influenced by the seductive system of the world. Prior to surrendering his life to the Lord, he engaged in unbridled acts of sexual immorality. His autographical book *Confessions* captures his youthful pleasures. Inflamed with passion, Augustine "could not wait patiently ... [and] was not a lover of marriage." He goes on to say, "I was a slave of my lust. And thus I began an affair with another woman."[5] In the book, Augustine confesses to living with an unnamed woman for many years.

In search of liberation from his sinful desires, Augustine turned to a friend named Simplicianus. In the course of discussion between the men, Simplicianus shared the story of the radical conversion of a man named Victorinus, in hopes of encouraging Augustine. His plan worked, for it eventually led to Augustine's decision to follow Christ. Victorinus's conversion deeply affected Augustine, motivating him to "glow with fervor to imitate him [Victorinus]."[6]

God used Ponticianus, another friend, to deliver the final nail in the coffin of the pre-regenerated Augustine. Ponticianus persuaded Augustine to pursue a life of monastic living removed from the world in order to serve Christ exclusively.

All resistance to surrendering to God was overcome by God's grace. Augustine prayed, "I was beside myself with madness that would bring me sanity." He continued: "I was dying a death that would bring me life."[7] With his former life behind him, he would later be baptized and discipled by Ambrose in Milan, who demonstrated that Christlike character is caught more than it's taught.

Subsequently, imitation was an integral part of Augustine's discipleship ministry, as he believed that ministry skills are cultivated through "informal apprenticeships and experience."[8] This is similar to the model practiced by Jesus: (1) lead while the disciples watch, (2) lead while the disciples assist, (3) assist while the disciples lead, and (4) watch while the disciples lead. Likewise,

Paul encouraged the Corinthian believers to "imitate" or "mimic" his life as he followed Jesus.

After returning to North Africa in 388, Augustine formed a community of committed believers in the town of Tagaste, where he had been born. Their purpose was to spur one another on to good works through mutual accountability, service, and the study of Scripture. Early in his ministry Augustine saw the need for discipleship relationships. While many monks secluded themselves in study and prayer, Augustine understood, contrary to many of his contemporaries, that spiritual growth flourishes in a group setting.

Augustine benefited from discipleship groups, a concept he learned from his time in the monastery at Hippo. "At each stage [of his ministry]," according to biographer Edward Smither, "he was the prime mover in bringing men together to pursue spiritual growth through disciplines such as prayer, psalm singing, reading, dialogue, work, and service."[9] Like John Wesley many years later, Augustine understood that holiness was to be pursued socially. The monastery afforded him the opportunity to live in community with other men for more than forty years.

The enactment of spiritual disciplines was the hallmark of Augustine's life, always done in a group setting — never alone. Accountability with other monks was a non-negotiable aspect of his personal spiritual growth. Members of his monastic community did more than pray privately (though they did that). Each person gathered daily with others for corporate prayer. Augustine implored the monks to bring others along on their journey, saying at one point, "Will he who makes good progress retreat so that he permits no human company at all?"[10]

Augustine rarely traveled alone. Whether defending the faith against opponents, wrestling with orthodoxy at church councils, or ministering to former Hippo alumni, he always brought a small group of disciples with him.[11] His sermons were seasoned with discipleship motifs. Smither identified four key themes in Augustine's preaching:

- The group must live together in unity
- The community itself is a means of spiritual growth
- Growth is facilitated by Christian friendship
- The group is a model for the church[12]

A final discipleship characteristic worth noting is Augustine's insatiable desire for self-development. As a lifelong learner, he was dissatisfied with mediocrity in his maturity. On one occasion he sent one of his disciples to spend time with Jerome, one of the most learned fathers of the Western Church, for the purpose of returning to teach Augustine what he discovered.[13] A great leader is a great learner. *The moment we stop learning, we cease leading.*

Augustine was a man who lived among the people. No matter the heights of his intellectual study, he never portrayed himself pretentiously before those he ministered to or lived with. One time he humbly told his congregation, "For you I am a Bishop, with you I am a Christian."[14] In this, he followed the example of the apostle Paul when he wrote to the church of Corinth:

> And I, when I came to you, brothers, did not come proclaiming to you the testimony of God with lofty speech or wisdom. For I decided to know nothing among you except Jesus Christ and him crucified. And I was with you in weakness and in fear and much trembling, and my speech and my message were not in plausible words of wisdom, but in demonstration of the Spirit and of power, so that your faith might not rest in the wisdom of men but in the power of God (1 Cor. 2:1–5 ESV).[15]

A Flame That Refused to Burn Out

The emphasis on communal living and discipleship was limited to monastic communities for many centuries after Augustine. Even though the task of making disciples was the primary focus of Jesus, the apostles, and some of the early Church Fathers, the elevation of the clergy and the loss of the doctrine of the priesthood of all believers led to a divide in the church and the neglect of discipleship. Heather Zempel, who leads the discipleship ministry at

National Community Church in Washington, DC, describes the model of the early church:

> The first model of discipleship that we see in history is the Relational model, which was the dominant approach to spiritual growth during the first few centuries of the church. It is built upon the premise that discipleship will occur naturally when Christians live in community with one another. Relational discipleship was vitally important during the early church because there was no New Testament and there were very few copies of Old Testament writings available to the common people. Spiritual truths were conveyed through the stories of the apostles and their letters to the churches.[16]

Unfortunately, what began as a grass roots, relational movement eventually turned into a structured hierarchy that quenched efforts at discipling those not pursuing professional ministry roles. The common understanding of the church changed from being a people to a place, from a body to a building. The ministry was seen as something done exclusively by the clergy, while the laity sat idle and took on a more passive role. Institutionalized ministry replaced individualized ministry.

Providentially, pockets of discipleship were preserved here and there during the centuries prior to the Reformation. Yet from the fifth century on, the work of discipleship was disparaged in the life of the average person in the church, at least in any intentional sense. With the split between laity and clergy, discipleship became a reality divorced from everyday life and the pursuit of those called to the monastic life. French historian and professor Alexandre Faivre comments,

> From this time onward, the layman's function was to release the priest and Levite from all his material concerns, thus enabling him to devote himself exclusively to the service of the altar, a task that was necessary for everyone's salvation.[17]

The Catholic Church still utilizes this clear divide between clergy and laity, with authority descending from the pope, in which only those trained are allowed to carry out the duties of ministry.

In the 1500s a monk named Martin Luther championed a reform movement in the Catholic Church, protesting against certain abuses and practices in the church. Luther became a proponent of the view that anyone could be equipped to read, study, and teach the Word of God, and he eventually translated the Bible into the German language for the common people. Luther argued that any believer could read and understand the Bible through the illumination of the Holy Spirit.

William Tyndale, an English scholar and a contemporary of Luther, shared this belief as well. English-speaking Christians in particular owe a debt of gratitude to Tyndale for the Bible we read today. In 1526, Tyndale was the first to translate the original Greek and Hebrew manuscripts into English. Much of Tyndale's work found its way into the King James Version less than a century later. Yet, instead of receiving praise for his diligent efforts, Tyndale was persecuted and arrested in 1535 and jailed in the castle of Vilvoorde outside Brussels for over a year. Later, he was tried for heresy and burned at the stake, all because he believed in offering the Bible in the vernacular of the common man.

A Book for Every Man

Luther may have constructed the vehicle for the Reformation by nailing his 95 Theses to the door of a church in Wittenberg, but it was Thomas Cranmer who paved the road for the journey to continue. Cranmer is the author of *The Book of Common Prayer*, one of the first devotional resources to gain widespread usage in the initial years of the Reformation. During his formative years, Cranmer possessed a voracious desire for learning. He was afforded the opportunity for an education in Cambridge, where he later joined other scholars to discuss Luther's theology and practices.

In August 1529, a chance conversation with King Henry VIII as he was visiting a neighboring community gave Cranmer the opportunity to use his writing and reasoning skills under the employ of the crown. King Henry was seeking to find biblical grounds to justify his divorce from his first wife, Catherine of Aragon, so he could marry his newfound love, Anne Boleyn. Cranmer was summoned by King Henry to write a letter to the papacy in favor of granting an annulment of King Henry's marriage. Rome denied the request, but this act earned Cranmer King Henry's respect, and he was appointed an ambassador of Europe. When the archbishop of Canterbury died three years later, Henry appointed Cranmer to assume the position of head of the Church of England.

Cranmer was now in a unique position to set a new direction for the English church. He called for reform among the clergy in his first work, the *Book of Homilies*, written in 1547. His second work, *Book of Common Prayer*, is what he is often remembered for today. The word "common" was used to describe the Scripture readings to be used for regular services. The book was a rubric for conducting church services, allowing for lectionary readings, songs, and creeds. It also contained outlines for performing weddings, funerals, and ordinations. Morning and evening prayers were included as well.

Today we struggle to fully grasp the impact this single book had on Christendom at the time it was published. In that day and age, few resources rivaled this book in popularity. Cranmer's emphasis on Scripture as the foundation for the weekly service was a significant detour from the structured formality of the Mass. The book soon became a standard resource among Protestants. And it was unique in that it was written in English. To this point most religious books were written in Latin, which few of the common people understood.

The Persecution of Bloody Mary

Although Cranmer believed that the king was God's chosen vessel to lead the church and the nation, and although he was loyal to King Henry, England would soon revert to a Catholic ruler under Queen Mary. Shortly after being crowned Queen of England, "Bloody Mary," as she was called, ordered the massacre of all protestant believers.[18] On June 10, 1540, Cranmer was arrested, stripped of his priestly office, and charged with treason for speaking out against the Catholic Church and the papacy. Believing that he could avoid being burned at the stake, Cranmer, weary from imprisonment, signed a document recanting his reformative stance against the Catholic Church. His signature appeared below a document stating:

> I confess and believe in one, holy, catholic visible church; I recognize as its supreme head upon earth the bishop of Rome, Pope and vicar of Christ, to whom all the faithful are bound subject. I beg and pray God to deign of his goodness to forgive me the faults I have committed against him and his church.

Additionally, he affirmed the seven sacraments, the original source of his repudiation against the church. Even though this denial contradicted everything he believed, it wasn't enough to save him from being sentenced to the stake. The government ordered his death, but only after one more confession, this time in public, in support of the Catholic Church. Weight of what he had done overwhelmed him immediately; it was too late to be saved from the flames. His own signature would be used to humiliate him throughout the region.

Although Cranmer's contributions continue to shape the Anglican Church (Church of England) today, they have come under some criticism as well. Some have criticized the formalized structure of the *Book of Common Prayer* as fostering spiritless leadership on the part of the minister and monotonous engagement on the part of the congregant. Yet these criticisms should be seen in light of the many positive contributions Cranmer made with the *Book of Common Prayer*, such as the emphasis on the pastoral prayer in the service.[19]

Puritan preacher and author William Perkins supported the practice of formal prayers as "being both profitable and necessary since they provide for uniformity in worship and prevent ignorant pastors from neglecting the duty of pastoral prayer."[20] More recently, J. I. Packer has captured the impact of Cranmer's efforts stating: "To make the Church of England a Bible-reading,

Bible-loving church was Cranmer's constant ideal."[21] While Cranmer's work was not necessarily the first "quiet time" devotional, it was certainly the most accessible for its time. Its simple language made it useful for the common man and became the go-to resource for personal devotion for countless believers around the world.

What Starts in the Home Spreads Through the Church

Another key leader who helped to recover the emphasis on discipleship among the common Christian was the Puritan writer and preacher Richard Baxter.

Baxter served for fourteen years as shepherd to the people at Kidderminster in England in the mid–1600s. Although he was imprisoned at the age of seventy for eighteen months (for libel), he remained unwaveringly true to his convictions. In addition to shepherding his own people, Baxter labored for unity among several Protestant denominations. He was instrumental in forming the Worcestershire Association of Ministers for the encouragement, edification, and accountability of his fellow pastors. He penned a comprehensive strategy for ministry, called *The Reformed Pastor*, a work that Charles Spurgeon would read two hundred years later to nurse his own spiritual malaise.

Spurgeon, the prolific preacher and influential pastor of the Metropolitan Tabernacle, once told his wife,

> I fear I have not been as faithful in my preaching today as I should have been; I have not been as much in earnest after poor souls as God would have me be.... Go, dear, to the study, and fetch down [Richard] Baxter's *Reformed Pastor*, and read some of it to me; perhaps that will quicken my sluggish heart.[22]

Baxter championed a *restorative* manner of ministry by insisting on the renewal of one's calling and motivation to administer the Word of God. Most significantly for our discussion, Baxter wasn't focused only on shepherding the flock, but on encouraging those in his flock to shepherd one another.

Baxter's disciple-making framework was shaped by his under-standing that belief drives behavior. He saw discipleship as more than just reading or passing along information; he emphasized the importance of understanding and applying theology for Christian nourishment and spiritual growth. He also connected his own pursuit of godliness to the task of making disciples. Every pastor, he believed, should be a disciple-maker.

Peter White, in his book *The Effective Pastor*, characterized Baxter's ministry as one of "the most spectacular growth in num-bers, and in the major features of true discipleship.... Baxter [had] a systematic approach to the detailed discipling of individuals."[23]

Reforming the Church

Baxter recognized that it was not only pastors who were entrusted with the responsibility of discipleship. One of Baxter's boldest be-liefs, shared by several of his contemporaries among the Puritans, is that the primary responsibility for discipleship in the home lay with Christian parents. He strongly urged fathers "of every fam-ily to cause his children and servants to repeat the Catechism to him, every Sabbath evening, and to give him some account of what they have heard at church during the day."[24] Worship in the homes consisted of reading Scripture and reciting and re-membering the catechisms of the faith. Baxter emphasized the necessity of family-based discipleship:

> We must have a special eye upon families, to see that they are well ordered, and the duties of each relation performed. The life of religion, and the welfare and glory of both the Church and the State, depend much on family government and duty. If we suffer the neglect of this, we shall undo all. I beseech you, there-fore, if you desire the reformation and welfare of your people, do all you can to promote family religion.[25]

At first glance, this emphasis on ministry in the home may not seem all that revolutionary, but we need to remember that much of this practice had been lost since the days of the early church. The father's role as spiritual mentor had largely been relegated to the local priest, and even in many Protestant homes fathers expected the pastor to facilitate and guide their shepherding and discipling duties.

Even though Baxter still believed that pastors are the key disciple-makers in the church, he was also clear in stating that they aren't the *only* ones. In expanding responsibility of discipleship into the home, Baxter was reinforcing the biblical teaching that discipleship is the responsibility of all believers. As he wrote, global reformation would not happen until "you procure family reformation. Some little religion there may be, here and there; but while it is confined to single persons, and is not promoted in families, it will not prosper, nor promise much future increase."[26]

This is a wonderful reminder to us that we cannot neglect our first ministry calling in our homes. This is equally true for pastors. A pastor must never sacrifice his family on the altar of ministry, no matter how fruitful or rewarding it may seem to be. What good is it if your church goes to heaven while your family heads to hell?

The Pursuit of Holiness Should Not Be Left to Chance

Following in the footsteps of the English Puritans, the American Jonathan Edwards was another pastor who emphasized the necessity of recovering practices of discipleship that would teach and equip the common man and woman. Edwards is often remembered for his sermon "Sinners in the Hands of an Angry God" and his impact on the First Great Awakening. According to historian Daniel Howe, Edwards exemplifies the American work ethic.[27] He consistently woke up between four or five in the morning to spend an average of thirteen hours a day in his study. He was serious about this, logging an entry in his journal on January 1728 justifying his regimen: "I think Christ has recommended rising early in the morning, by his rising from the grave very early."[28]

For Edwards, a disciplined life was an act of worship to God. "In addition to carefully crafting lengthy sermons each week, he was deeply engaged in biblical study, a daily activity that produced several major notebooks filled with his tiny writing."[29] Over the course of his life, Edwards authored fourteen books and produced hundreds of sermons, many of which are still read and studied today.

One of his writings is a list of "resolutions," a God-centered pattern for structuring one's life into a system for spiritual growth and accountability. The first resolution on Edwards's list encompasses his life's goals:

> Resolved that I will do whatsoever I think to be most to God's glory, and my own good, profit and pleasure, in the whole of my duration, without any consideration of the time, whether now, or never so many myriads of ages hence.
>
> ———
>
> Resolved to do whatever I think to be my duty and most for the good and advantage of mankind in general. Resolved to do this, whatever difficulties I meet with, how many and how great soever.[30]

In the area of time management, Edwards "resolved, never to lose one moment of time; but improve it the most profitable way I possibly can." Also, "never to do anything, which I should be afraid to do, if it were the last hour of my life." Edwards was militant in decimating wasted time in his Christian walk. Resolution 48 states, "Resolved, constantly, with the utmost niceness and diligence, and the strictest scrutiny, to be looking into the state of my soul, that I may know whether I have truly an interest in Christ or no; that when I come to die, I may not have any negligence respecting this to repent of."[31] Edwards knew that *you can't expect from others what you don't emulate yourself.* Therefore, he militantly practiced what he preached.

What is the value of studying Edwards' resolutions as we look at rediscovering discipleship for the church today? Consider how different our lives would be if we had our own list of declarations. What if we established goals for spiritual growth and followed them, not out of coercion or compulsion, but as a response to the received grace of God? While we need to avoid the dangerous trap of legalism, there is great value in thinking through clear goals and developing strategies for spiritual growth. Edwards was strongly convinced of the sovereignty of God over his life, yet he also resolved not to leave his spiritual growth to chance, taking responsibility for it through specific actions.

In conclusion, this brief journey through the history of discipleship provides an important context for our own attempt to *rediscover* discipleship. Each historical figure offers a fundamental aspect of discipleship that we overlook to our own peril. Augustine, for example, represents an early paradigm for discipleship. His convictions are only partially recovered by Reformers such as Luther and Tyndale, following a medieval era characterized, among other things, by a gulf between clergy and laity. It was Cranmer, however, who made tangible progress in closing this gap with his emphasis on Bible study and his *Book of Common Prayer*. Later Puritans, such as Richard Baxter, built upon his legacy by reinforcing the biblical teaching that discipleship is the responsibility of all believers. Jonathan Edwards represents, perhaps, a high point in church history with his list of "resolutions," a God-centered pattern for structuring his life into a system for spiritual growth and accountability.

Observing these examples of Christian men from years past motivates us to take a bold step forward for God. Church history offers the contemporary reader a bit of momentum. When we peer back through time, we are propelled forward. Paul in 1 Corinthians 10:11 illustrates this point: "Now these things happened to them as examples, and they were written as a warning to us, on whom the ends of the ages have come." A study of church history also gives us a front row seat to the unfolding of God's redemptive plan throughout the ages. Iain Campbell, in his book *Heroes and Heretics*, suggests, "The events of this world's history set the stage upon which the drama of redemption is enacted."[32]

One English preacher was so formative throughout the First Great Awakening that he deserves special treatment. Although he is widely known for his preaching, John Wesley was an organizational genius of collaboration. It is his single-minded passion to make disciples that we consider in the next chapter.

CHAPTER 6

A Band-Aid for the Church

EVEN CASUAL CONVERSATIONS WITH OTHER pastors inevitably turn to the increasingly crucial topic of discipleship. I recall a conversation with a fellow pastor of a well-known megachurch who shared how he was personally discipling a group of men in his church, though he admitted that beyond that group, disciple-making was virtually nonexistent. His executive pastor was with us, and he added his own understanding of how to go about making disciples: "Discipleship should be organic and not intentional. It should not be planned or prepared."

"Unfortunately, Jesus never left discipleship to chance," was my simple reply. "He was intentional and calculative from the beginning." In fact, as Jesus discipled the twelve men who would change the world, he gradually released them into ministry through a definitive four-step process.

First, Jesus ministered while the disciples watched.

Second, Jesus allowed the disciples to assist him in ministry.

Third, the disciples ministered with Jesus' assistance.

Finally, Jesus observed as the disciples ministered to others.

This was Jesus' model for discipleship then, and it continues to be his plan for discipleship today. If Jesus had a model and a plan, shouldn't we have one?

A Method for Making Disciples

In the previous chapter we saw that over the past five hundred years, since the time of the Reformation, there has been a gradual recovery of the importance of discipleship as the core mission of the church. While many notable figures have contributed to this recovery, perhaps no single individual has had an impact as large as that of John Wesley. While many are familiar with Wesley's dynamic preaching, they are usually unaware of his tenacious pursuit of a prescriptive process for making disciples out of believers.[1] Wesley is one of those rare individuals who was an equally brilliant evangelist for the masses and scrupulous discipler for the individual. Early Methodist James Hall, in his autobiography, identified the method for personal spiritual development that Wesley devised as the one factor that "greatly helped me [move] forward in the ways of God."[2]

Malcolm Gladwell, in his book *The Tipping Point*, points out the significance of John Wesley's ministry by comparing him to several others of his time:

> But Methodism's founder, John Wesley, was by no means the most charismatic preacher of his era. That honor belonged to George Whitefield, an orator of such power and charisma that, it was said, he once charmed a five-pound contribution out of Benjamin Franklin — who was, of course, the furthest thing from a churchgoer. Nor was Wesley a great theologian, in the tradition of, say, John Calvin or Martin Luther. His genius was organizational. Wesley would travel around England and North America delivering open-air sermons to thousands of people. But he didn't just preach. He also stayed long enough in each town to form the most enthusiastic of his converts into religious societies, which in turn he subdivided into smaller classes of a dozen or so people.[3]

Wesley was, by all accounts, an organizational mastermind. And while Wesley's doctrines may have the propensity to divide, his methods for making disciples have invariably been unifying.[4] He was an organizational genius who initiated a movement that was, at one point, the largest Protestant denomination in America.

The most bountiful fruits of Wesley's labor, however, would come after his death. According to historian Kevin Watson,

From 1776 to 1850 American Methodists grew like a weed. In 1776, Methodists accounted for 2.5 percent of religious adherents in the colonies, the second smallest of the major denominations of that time. By 1850, Methodists comprised 34.2 percent of religious adherents in the United States, which was 14 percent more than the next largest group.[5]

Through a brief survey, what is most striking is his dedication to developing a prescriptive method for spiritual growth. Wesley had a zeal for the lost and desired nothing more than to spread the gospel. Preaching more than 44,000 times, Wesley averaged an incredible three sermons a day for fifty-four years. In doing this, he traveled more than 200,000 miles by horseback and carriage, which amounts to about 5,000 miles a year.[6] He devoted his entire life to the Lord, even repeating the words of Isaac Watts' hymn, "I'll praise my maker, while I've breath," before he died.[7]

The Holy Club

John Wesley was the fifteenth child in a family of nineteen children. His family was far from typical. Both of his parents, Samuel and Susannah, were held in high esteem, and their social standing and wealth afforded him the opportunity to attend both the prestigious Charter House School and Oxford University, two of the finest institutions in England.

At the age of ten, Wesley began schooling in London, and even at a young age he felt deeply convicted about his inward spiritual life. In his writing, he recalls these years at the Charter House as his "rebellious phase." Biographer Stephen Tompkins says of this stage in Wesley's life: "He still read the Bible and said his prayers evening and morning, and his behavior seemed to be exemplar. Nevertheless, in the light of his evangelical conversion, he remembered this time as a fall from grace."[8] Wesley felt that he had slacked in his commitment to the Lord during his younger school years, so at the age of sixteen he left London to attend Oxford University.

At Oxford, Wesley immersed himself in the study of spiritual writings and soon felt his life dramatically change. His own words provide insight into his new perspective on ministry:

> In the year of 1725, being in the twenty-third year of my age, I met with Bishop Taylor's, *Rules and Exercises of Holy Living and Dying*. In reading several parts of this book, I was exceedingly affected by that part in particular, which related to "purity and intention." Instantly, I resolved to dedicate all my life to God, all my thoughts, and all my words, being thoroughly convinced there was no medium but that every part of my life must either be a sacrifice to God or to me.[9]

A group on campus called the Cambridge Platonists insisted that the inward world of spirituality mattered more than outward display, and Wesley was influenced by this group.[10] This period at Oxford led him to start the Holy Club with his brother Charles and his good friend George Whitefield. The club was quite fond of reading the writings of Thomas à Kempis, Jeremy Taylor, and William Law. In addition to reading the classics, members of the Holy Club engaged in long periods of prayer, seasons of fasting, daily time for Bible reading, confession of sins, and routine observance of the sacraments.

Club members were expected to adhere strictly and methodically to religious precepts and practices. They visited prisons, evangelized the lost, comforted the sick, and served others in order to avoid pharisaic comparison and to maintain consistency between their inward and outward spirituality. To the members of the Holy Club, faith without works was lifeless.

The disciplined nature of the club garnered scorn from outsiders, who began referring to the group as "Methodists" because of their methodical approach to the Christian life.[11] Yet the pejorative "Methodist" label stuck and was eventually embraced by Wesley and the other members. The club defined the common principles of Christianity and, in turn, exemplified what the Christian life should look like.

From Georgia State to Aldersgate

In July 1735, Dr. John Burton, Trustee of the Georgia Colony in the United States and patron of the Society for the Propagation of the Gospel, invited Wesley to transfer the Holy Club to Georgia to help local missionaries reach the Indians.[12] Wesley accepted the offer in September, but unfortunately only four members of the club were able to make the trip with him to Georgia. Wesley, his brother Charles, Benjamin Ingham, and Charles Delamotte sailed from Gravesend to Georgia in October 1735. George Whitefield remained behind with the intention of joining the group at a later time.

Tompkins says,

> Wesley's motive for going to Georgia was simple: to save his soul. In the back-to-basics society of the settlement, away from the demands of modern life and the distraction of womankind, he would have a chance to pursue the goal that eluded him in Oxford — the unhampered practice of holiness and the holy molding of others.[13]

In order to remain focused, the team fasted often and spent long periods in concentrated prayer. Unexpectedly, however, Wesley fell in love with a woman named Sophie Hopkey. This relationship failed, and it greatly affected his focus, ultimately landing him on a ship headed back to England after just three years of service.

On the return voyage to England, Wesley was downcast, lamenting what he felt was an unsuccessful ministry in the American colonies. His ambition to convert Indians had little result, with only a few spiritual conversations. Wesley began to question his own purpose and calling in life.[14] After returning to England in February, he surprised his friend, Whitefield, who was making his own preparations to join Wesley's team in America. Wesley declined Whitefield's invitation to return to the States.

After Whitefield left to advance the ministry in the Colonies, Wesley continued to struggle with his calling and even had doubts about his own salvation. Peter Bohler, someone he met on the trip to Georgia, identified faults in Wesley's faith, insisting that a works-based salvation is insufficient for attaining eternal life. Conversations like these cracked open the door for Wesley's transformative encounter on May 24, 1738. On that day Wesley recalls listening to a reading of Luther's preface to the Epistle of Romans at St. Paul's Cathedral on Aldersgate Street. As he heard the words "the change which God works in the heart through faith in Christ," Wesley experienced a holy conviction and put his trust in Christ as Savior.[15] Wesley confirmed his salvation in the Lord at St. Paul's Cathedral.

Basil Miller comments, "Judged by the products of Wesley's life, Aldersgate stands by far as the brightest spot in his life or in the life of anyone of his century. Before Aldersgate, he was a bungler; after Aldersgate, he was a lion in God's kingdom who knew no defeat."[16] Until that moment in St. Paul's Cathedral, Wesley's preaching was largely uninspired and unsuccessful. Afterward, his preaching was imbued with holy fire, lit by the assurance of his faith in Christ.

Unity in the Community

Given the background of the Cambridge Platonists, his own personal evangelistic failures, and his experience at Aldersgate, it makes sense that Wesley became a founder of a prescriptive approach to disciple-making. But this approach did not originate with him. Beginning with men like Martin Luther, Phillip Jacob Spener, August Hermann Francke, and Nikolaus Ludwig von Zinzendorf, the idea of transformational small groups had begun to form in the Protestant church.

Spener, known today as the Father of Pietism, established what he called *collegia pietatis*, or "gatherings for piety." He insisted on individual Bible study and personal development — a practice countercultural at the time and strongly discouraged by the papacy.

Going against the Catholic practice of one-on-one confession to a priest, Spener insisted that truths learned from Scripture are meant to be lived out in a community. Spener despised individualism, claiming that "it acted like a medicine which was more dangerous than the disease it was supposed to cure."[17] In his classic contribution, *Pia Desideria*, he outlined six actions for enacting reform in the church, all of which focused on developing more mature and devoted members of the church through intensive, deep individual growth cultivated in the arena of community.

One of his students took Spener's insights in the *Pia Desideria* and put them into practice, starting a community intentionally focused on discipleship and missions. The student, Nikolaus von Zinzendorf — or Count Zinzendorf, as he was known to the Moravian community to which he ministered in Herrnhut — taught that "the way to restore and revitalize ecclesiastical organization was the proliferation of independent renewal groups within the official framework of the larger organization. This was known among most pious as the 'ecclesiae in the ecclesia.'"[18]

Count Zinzendorf became a crucial player in the mobilization of believers. Sixty years before William Carey went to India and 150 years before Hudson Taylor ministered in China, Zinzendorf began sending out missionaries to St. Thomas Island in the West Indies. Over the next 150 years, the Moravian brotherhood sent out more than 2,000 missionaries.

Wesley caught wind of Zinzendorf's incredibly successful missionary mobilization and what he learned struck a chord deep in his spirit. He recalled his own failed missionary expedition to the American colonies and traveled to meet the count shortly after confirming his faith in Christ at Aldersgate. His goal was to evaluate the community operation, which at the time had been active for almost eleven years. Wesley was struck by the certain confidence the Moravians had in the sovereignty of God, and by how well they composed themselves in the midst of storms at sea. He recorded one particular incident in his journal:

> In the midst of the psalm wherewith their service began the sea broke over, split the mainsail in pieces, covered the ship, and poured in between the decks, as if the great deep had already swallowed us up. A terrible screaming began among the English.

The Germans [Moravians] calmly sung on. I asked one of them afterwards, "Was you not afraid?" He answered, "I thank God, no." I asked, "But were your women and children afraid?" He replied mildly, "No; our women and children are not afraid to die."[19]

The trip to Hernhutt first opened Wesley's eyes to authentic biblical community, giving him a taste of the fruit that discipleship could produce. Wesley documented several different groups represented among the Moravians: "The people of Herrnhut are divided" ...

1. Into five male classes and five female classes.

2. Into eleven classes, according to the houses where they live. And in each class is a helper, an overseer, a monitor, an almoner, and a servant.

3. Into about ninety bands, each of which meets twice a week at least, but most of them three times a week, to "confess their faults one to another, and pray for one another, that they may be healed."[20]

Wesley was particularly struck by how the Moravians' group dynamic intentionally moved people closer to Christ. This led to his own creation of a three-step disciple-making process. Wesley worked so passionately at developing and perfecting this process that one biographer later described him as the "master of minutiae."[21] Eventually John Wesley, seasoned by his failed attempt at ministry and his newfound assurance of salvation, was able to realize on a massive scale what the Moravians had done so well in their community.

Societies, Classes, and Bands

Elton Trueblood, a noted twentieth-century theologian, once commented on the central problem facing the church, even as the membership rolls grew in number: a profound lack of involvement and the lack of serious commitment to the mission of Christ:

Perhaps the greatest single weakness of the contemporary Christian Church is that millions of supposed members are not really involved at all and, what is worse, do not think it strange that they are not. As soon as we recognize Christ's intention to make His Church a militant company, we understand at once that the conventional arrangement cannot suffice. There is no real chance of victory in a campaign if ninety percent of the soldiers are untrained and uninvolved, but that is exactly where we stand now.[22]

The problems Trueblood mentions are nothing new, as we have seen in our survey of church history. And in his own encounters with the Moravians, Wesley recognized the crucial need for organization among the followers of Christ, lest they be, as Jesus put it, "harassed and helpless, like sheep without a shepherd" (Matt. 9:36 NIV). Wesley separated those who joined his Methodist movement into "'connection' [groups], and a number of societies [were separated] into a 'circuit' under the leadership of a 'superintendent.'"[23]

When asked during the early years of the Methodist movement why he didn't focus his attention on preaching and allow God to look after the converts, Wesley responded, "We have made the trial in various places … but in all [of them] the seed has fallen by the highwayside. There is scarce any fruit remaining."[24]

Wesley's disciple-making innovation was to view the stages of spiritual growth in a conveyor belt-like progression, occurring through groups. Wesley organized people into three sections, with each one progressing into the next. *Societies* were the largest groups, which he subdivided into *classes*, which he then broke down into what he called *bands*. Two other related groups, though not as prominent, were created to meet specific needs: *Select Societies* were for training individuals in specialized areas, and *Penitent Bands* were for dealing with cases of addiction and behavior issues. The Penitent Bands functioned as a sort of precursor to ministries such as Alcoholics Anonymous and Celebrate Recovery.

The Society had the least stringent rules for membership and participation. Societies were similar to what we might today call congregations. Together the people learned, worshiped, and grew in their faith, but the Society was simply the first step on the journey to grow in godliness.

The Class had membership based on certain non-negotiable behavioral criteria. Classes required their members to attend regularly and to actively participate. An individual could not attend the Class meetings and refuse to contribute. Wesley kept track of members in good standing by issuing tickets — small cards bearing the member's name.[25] New tickets were issued periodically so that members were prevented from attending without a quarterly evaluation.

Societies and Classes moved people toward Bands, the final stage in Wesley's disciple-making process. D. Michael Henderson summarizes the distinctions between the three stages: "It could be said metaphorically that the society aimed for the head, the class meeting for the hands, and the band for the heart."[26] Each of these three phases in a new member's spiritual development was specifically tailored for the steps one would take on the Christian journey toward maturity: deliverance from sin and cognition of Jesus as Lord, equipping the Christian for being the hands and feet of the gospel, and anchoring his or her heart with other believers who may sharpen one another.

Wesley pushed against the normal means of character development in his day, which encouraged pursuing personal, affective change before social. It was largely based on the idea that belief drives behavior, that when the will is changed, the right behavior will follow. Instead, Wesley believed that when a person changed their behavior or actions, they would *simultaneously* improve their character. The popular saying "Fake it 'til you make it" may have found its roots in this line of thinking.

This is a rare band ticket from my personal collection.

Wesley preferred that the Classes be limited to between seven and twelve members, although in practice the Class sizes tended to be much larger. Both men and women of various ages attended these smaller gatherings for growth in holiness. The purpose of a Class meeting was not to gather more information. Rather, members met to apply and reflect on the messages they had heard in the public Society meetings. In essence, these were the first sermon-based small groups. Attendance in the Society was not optional if one wanted to continue in the Class, and participation through honest and open sharing was expected.

Accelerated Growth Groups

The final stage of discipleship, the Bands, were where the "message moved from print to voice, from individualism to community, from cognition to emotion, and from private to public."[27] These groups focused on attuning each participant to the heart of Christ. The demands of these groups were rigorous and attendance was voluntary. These were always gender-specific groups and they met at least once a week, though many gathered multiple times a week for personal accountability and encouragement.

There were several key questions proposed to every potential member before he or she was admitted to the group each week:

1. Have you the forgiveness of your sins?

2. Have you peace with God through our Lord Jesus Christ?

3. Have you the witness of God's Spirit with your spirit, that you are a child of God?

4. Is the love of God shed abroad in your heart?

5. Has no sin, inward or outward, dominion over you?

6. Do you desire to be told your faults?

7. Do you desire to be told of all your faults, and that plain and home?

8. Do you desire that every one of us should tell you, from time to time, whatsoever is in his heart concerning you?

9. Consider! Do you desire we should tell you whatsoever we think, whatsoever we fear, whatsoever we hear, concerning you?

10. Do you desire that, in doing this, we should come as close as possible, that we should cut to the quick, and search your heart to the bottom?

11. Is it your desire and design to be on this, and all other occasions, entirely open, so as to speak everything that is in your heart without exception, without disguise, and without reserve?[28]

Above all else, honesty, confidentiality, and trust were paramount. In addition to the periodic reiteration of these foundational questions, four more personal probings were made weekly: What known sins have you committed since our last meeting? What temptations have you met with? How were you delivered? What have you thought, said, or done, of which you doubt whether it be sin or not?

Bands were exclusive, closed groups. Unbelievers were excluded from participating in a Band, hence its position at the end of Wesley's discipleship process. Kevin Watson, a historian well versed in Wesley's practice of discipleship, elaborates on the stringent prerequisites for joining: "Prospective members were expected to have previously experienced justification by faith and to have assurance of their adoption as children of God."[29]

Participation in the Band was available only to born-again believers because its purpose was to pursue social holiness, something an unbeliever was incapable of doing.[30] Wesley also made sure to foster individual commitment, issuing a warning to those who viewed the gatherings nonchalantly: "Never omit meeting your Class or Band; never absent yourself from any public meeting. These are the very sinews of our Society; and whatever weakens, or tends to weaken, our regard for these, or our exactness in attending them, strikes at the very root of our community."[31]

Applying Wesley's Model Today

At Brainerd Baptist Church, we have taken Wesley's model and created a Discipleship Pathway for believers to embark on: Congregation (Societies), Community (Classes), and Core (Bands)—see Figure 1.[32] Members are asked to consider where they are in the pipeline of spiritual growth in order to take the next step of their journey.

The Congregation (50+ people) is a weekly worship gathering, typically on Sunday morning. The purpose is to engage in a time of celebration through prayer, singing, study of the Scriptures, and love for one another. The Community group (15–20 people), often a Bible study or small group, meets for behavioral change. The Core group, or D-Group, consists of gender specific groups of 3 to 5 for the purpose of commitment and accountability. (I unpack this concept in chapter 9.)

FIGURE 1—The 3-Strand Church Model: The Master's Plan for Discipleship			
Jesus' Model	Multitudes	The 12	The 3 (Peter, James, John)
Wesley's Model	Societies	Classes	Bands
3-Strand Model	Congregation	Community	Core
Group Size	50+	8–20	3–5
Focus	Celebration	Community/Fellowship	Commitment
Population	Mixed gender	Mostly mixed gender	Gender specific
Message Content	General	Less general	Discipleship Specific

Discipleship Convictions

What made Wesley's three-fold model so effective was its inherently practical nature. In addition to cognitive learning, Wesley emphasized learning through experience. He lived by four basic discipleship convictions:

1. The necessity of discipleship: "I am more convinced that the devil himself desires nothing more than this, that the people of any place (any church) should be half-awakened and then left to themselves to fall asleep again."

2. The necessity of small groups for discipleship: his three-strand process of Societies, Classes, and Bands.

3. The necessity of leadership in discipleship: Wesley trained and mobilized a massive army of leaders, putting as many as ten of his members, who were from all walks of life, into leadership roles.

4. Holiness and service as the goals of discipleship: the people produced through Wesley's system reformed both the church and the society in which they lived.[33]

What set Wesley and his followers apart from the other religious groups surrounding them was that "many church leaders were telling people what they *ought* to do, but the Methodists were telling each other what they were *doing*."[34] Francis Asbury encapsulates the purpose of the Band when he writes, "We have no doubt, but meetings of Christian brethren for the exposition of scripture-texts may be attended with their advantages. But the most profitable exercise of any is a free inquiry into the state of the heart."[35]

Bearing Fruit That Lasts

As we saw earlier, Wesley and his friend George Whitefield were, at one point, united for spiritual renewal during their time at Oxford. Yet over time, doctrinal differences polarized their long-time relationship.[36] Whitefield also went on to have a profoundly successful preaching ministry and was instrumental in the First Great Awakening in the American Colonies. In addition to their doctrinal differences, the two men also disagreed on how to follow up with men and women who responded to the preaching of the Word. As one historian explains, "Whitefield hoped that those who had been 'awakened' would follow through on their own initiative; Wesley left nothing to chance. He made sure that those who were serious about leading a new life were channeled into small groups for growth in discipleship."[37]

Whitefield agreed with Wesley that it was necessary for new converts to get connected to the church, but he failed to implement anything akin to the Wesleyan discipleship model. Historically, his ministry proved less effective in assimilation than Wesley's. Nineteenth-century historian Holland McTyeire says of their different approaches,

> It was by this means [the formation of Societies] that we have been enabled to establish permanent and holy churches over the world. Mr. Wesley saw the necessity of this from the beginning. Mr. Whitefield, when he separated from Mr. Wesley, did not follow it. What was the consequence? The fruit of Mr. Whitefield died with himself. Mr. Wesley's fruit remains, grows, increases, and multiplies exceedingly.[38]

Even though Whitefield and Wesley continued to disagree on key matters of doctrine until their deaths, Whitefield later regretted his failure to adopt Wesley's organizational insights in his own ministry. John Pool, a Methodist pastor, recalls a conversation with Whitefield about this:

Whitefield: Well, John, art thou still a Wesleyan?

Pool: Yes, sir. I thank God I have the privilege of being in connection with Mr. Wesley, and one of his preachers.

Whitefield: John, thou art in thy right place. My brother Wesley acted wisely; the souls that were awakened under his ministry he joined in class, and thus preserved the fruits of his labor. This I neglected, and my people are a rope of sand.[39]

Both Whitefield and Wesley were blessed by God to be instruments of revival. But because his ministry lacked organizational and institutional structure, the fruit of Whitefield's ministry died with himself. By contrast, Mr. Wesley's fruit remained, grew, and multiplied for several generations.[40] Because he wisely utilized organizational methods, Methodism didn't die with John Wesley. It continued to grow under his disciples long after his death.

CHAPTER 7

A Comma That May Have Kept the Church in a Discipleship Coma

PUNCTUATION MARKS ARE IMPORTANT. In the wrong place, a simple mark can lead to a devastating misunderstanding. Take these two sentences, for example:

> "Let's eat Grandpa!"

> "Let's eat, Grandpa!"

Notice that the comma makes a big difference — especially if you are Grandpa!

Here is another example to make my point. Recently, Goodwill posted a sign outside its building:

> "Thank you! Your donation just helped someone. Get a job."

Obviously, the insertion of that first period makes a difference. What they likely meant to communicate was:

> "Thank you! Your donation just helped someone get a job."

One punctuation mark, either inserted or excluded, has the potential to change the meaning of an entire sentence.

During the process of obtaining endorsements for a book I had written, I spoke with several pastors who admitted that they had minimized or neglected the process of making disciples. One told me, "For years our goal was to get them to church and get them saved."

Another said, "Success in ministry was determined by how many parents could drag — I mean 'bring' — their children to Sunday school." Discipleship was clearly not the bull's-eye on their ministerial target. For several, it had no place on the target whatsoever!

So why are we just now catching on to the importance of discipleship?

I think I may have the answer.

Just as a single comma can change the fate of Grandpa in the example above, a single comma has paralyzed believers in the Christian church for nearly four hundred years. As we saw in our historical tour in the previous chapters, the chasm between clergy and the laity has been narrowing since the Reformation five hundred years ago. Yet it has not narrowed enough. Some of that may be due to the influence of the 1611 King James Version of the Bible.

A Bible for Everyone

A few years ago I began collecting Bible leaves, copies of actual Bibles that have survived the ravages of time, typically sold for exuberant amounts of money. Much as dealers sell baseball cards or comic books, people sell single pages of Bibles that have fallen out of the original book. Thanks to the wonders of the Internet, specific pages can be acquired through some savvy searching. Eventually my persistence paid off, and I was able to acquire a copy of an original page from a 1611 King James Version "He" Bible. (The "He" version, as opposed to the "She," is the first printed copy.) The leaf on which the page is printed is nothing special. The story behind the leaf, however, is entertaining and revealing.

Richard Bancroft, a former Archbishop of Canterbury, was a staunch critic of Puritanism and the *Geneva Bible*, the Bible translated and annotated by several of the Reformers. Bancroft encouraged King James to consider developing his own translation. At the time, three versions were in circulation: the *Great Bible*, the *Bishops' Bible*, and the *Geneva Bible*. The first two were authorized by the Church of England and preferred by the clergy, although the *Great* was losing ground to the newer *Bishops'*.

The *Geneva*, on the other hand, was a favorite among the masses as well as the Puritan leaders in the Church of England. Even though the *Geneva* was a superior translation, the Church rejected it because of its anti-monarchical annotations. The stage was set, then, for a new translation.

Fifty-four of England's foremost Bible scholars (although only forty-seven are mentioned by name in the printed copy) were divided into six panels — two at Oxford, two at Cambridge, and two at Westminster. The translation was to be a revision of the *Bishops' Bible*. Words that were omitted by William Tyndale were reintroduced: "church" in place of "congregation," and "charity" instead of "love." After the translation was complete, a committee of twelve convened, comprised of two scholars from each of the six panels. The fourteen apocryphal books were included in the completed version, as they had been in the previous authorized English Bibles. It took the members of this committee three years of nonstop work to present a finished, printed translation. They spent another three years reviewing the translation and an additional nine months to prepare it for the press. The result was the original 1611 King James Version.

The 1611 lasted for over a hundred years until author Hugh Ross called for a revision of the 1611 KJV in 1727. John Wesley introduced his own revision of the KJV in 1755, making more than 12,000 changes. Benjamin Blayney's 1769 Oxford Standard Edition of the KJV is essentially the version that is still printed today. Blayney's edition is estimated to differ from the original 1611 version in at least 75,000 details.[1] The current KJV available in most bookstores today differs from the original in that in omits the fourteen apocryphal books. Originally, the punishment for their exclusion, according to the Archbishop of Canterbury, was one-year imprisonment.

The Comma in Contention

Why all of this background on the King James? Well, if you examine the KJV translation of Ephesians 4:11–13, you will find two

commas in verse 12, commas that significantly alter our understanding of the verse. The verse reads:

> And he gave some, apostles; and some, prophets; and some,
> evangelists; and some, pastors and teachers; For the perfecting of
> the saints, [COMMA] for the work of the ministry, [COMMA]
> for the edifying of the body of Christ: Till we all come in the
> unity of the faith, and of the knowledge of the Son of God, unto
> a perfect man, unto the measure of the stature of the fulness of
> Christ.

So let me ask you. Based on what you've just read, what is the
job of the apostles, prophets, evangelists, pastors, and teachers?
Many would say that it is threefold:

1. to perfect the saints,

2. to do the work of the ministry, and

3. to edify the body of Christ.

According to the KJV translation, the ministers, pastors, and
trained professionals are expected to carry out all the ministerial
duties.

Now, for those who learned Greek in school, you already
know that the original documents are devoid of punctuation
marks, particularly anything like our commas in English. The insertion of punctuation is based on the judgment of the translator.
I am convinced that this comma may be largely to blame for the
discipleship coma of the church for the past four hundred years.

The thinking reflected in the KJV translation of Ephesians
4 is prominent in many churches today. Author and pastor Larry Osborne has labeled it "the Holy Man Myth." According to
Osborne,

> "The Holy Man Myth" is the idea that pastors and clergy some-
> how have a more direct line to God. It cripples a church because
> it overburdens pastors and underutilizes the gifts and anointing
> of everyone else. It mistakenly equates leadership gifts with su-
> perior spirituality.[2]

Left uncorrected, this paradigm will paralyze laypeople and rob the congregation of ministerial blessings.

So how does the Greek text of Ephesians 4:11–13 actually read? The vast majority of modern translations, including the English Standard Version, remove the comma. Here's how the English Standard Version reads:

> And he gave the apostles, the prophets, the evangelists, the shepherds and teachers, to equip the saints [NO COMMA] for the work of ministry, for building up the body of Christ, until we all attain to the unity of the faith and of the knowledge of the Son of God, to mature manhood, to the measure of the stature of the fullness of Christ.

Notice how this changes the flow of the passage. The job of pastors, mentors, and leaders is not to do the work of ministry or build up the body as something apart from the equipping of the saints. It is the job of pastors and leaders to equip believers to carry out *their* God-given ministry. The effectiveness of a pastor is not gauged by the performance of his ministerial duties alone, but by how well they develop other disciples, preachers, pastors, godly fathers, and Christ-honoring students. Harold Hoehner summarizes the meaning of this passage:

> In brief, the point is that the gifted persons listed in verse 11 serve as the foundational gifts that are used for the immediate purpose of preparing all the saints to minister. Thus, every believer must do the work of ministry.[3]

To put it simply: *Ministry is the pathway to maturity*, not the other way around.

Teach All Nations or Make Disciples of All Nations?

The King James Version's prominence, I believe, is one of the reasons why there has been such a glaring lack of discipleship over the last four centuries — and this is partly due to another translation choice. The KJV renders the Greek word for "make disciples" as "teach." So Matthew 28:19 reads, "Go ye therefore, and *teach* all nations...." Today almost all modern versions translate the verb *matheteuo* as "make disciples" instead of "teach." Even the New King James Version states, "Go therefore and *make disciples* of all the nations."

So is there a difference between "teaching" and "making disciples"? I believe there is. Many diligent believers have read this as a command to "teach" people about salvation. They take this to mean that they share the gospel and then encourage people to "ask Jesus into their hearts." They communicate information. But while communicating information is important, discipleship doesn't end there. As we learned in our study of the Hebraic roots of discipleship, more is required to make a disciple than knowing facts about Jesus. Making disciples requires equipping and investing in a lengthy training process, particularly for new believers.

Consider an example. Imagine that you received a note from your father about lawn care for his yard. "Go to the garage, take out the lawn mower, weed-eater, and blower. Bring each of them to the front yard. Finally, fill the lawn mower up with gas. Have this done before I get home from work."

What will Dad find when he pulls into the driveway after work? He will see uncut grass, clean machines, and a relaxed son.

When your father asks, "Why didn't you mow the grass?" and "Why didn't you edge the curb with the weed-eater?" and "Why didn't you use the blower?" what will be your response?

"Because you didn't tell me to do that!"

Perhaps one of the reasons why we haven't seen an emphasis on discipleship at the forefront of our ministries is that many have gone to the nations simply to "teach" — not to disciple.

Now, I know that some of you are objecting at this point: "Isn't teaching really synonymous with making disciples?"

Well, yes and no. Teaching is a part of discipleship, but discipleship involves far more than teaching. Bill Hull, a leader in personally obeying the Great Commission, has sounded the clarion call for discipleship over the past twenty years. Hull rightly insists that understanding "what a disciple is and what a disciple does are top priorities for the church."[4] He adds that many churches are carelessly guilty of throwing "the word disciple around freely, but too often with no definition."[5]

At the very core, a disciple is a learner, one who is set on growing and developing. In nearly every sphere of life, people learn specific skills from someone else who has developed those skills. An electrical certification is attained only after an extensive apprenticeship with a more experienced electrician. When a prospective doctor finishes medical school, she invests several years in a residency, a time of shadowing an experienced physician.

If a psychiatrist bases his practice on the teachings of Sigmund Freud, we might say he is "a disciple of Freud." If a musician, following the methods of Wynton Marsalis, plays jazz in the same style, we might comment that he is "a disciple of Wynton Marsalis." This concept of learning directly through the expertise and experience of another is the foundation of what Jesus envisioned when He used the term "disciple." So how does this understanding of the word *matheteuo*, or "make disciples," affect how we live our Christian lives?

"Disciple" is a dynamic term for a "learner" or "student" who actively learns, through hearing and practice, the teaching of his or her teacher. A disciple is one who "is intentionally equipped with the Word of God through accountable relationships that are empowered by the Holy Spirit in order to produce Christ-likeness."[6] At the core, a disciple is not one who is in a static state of being, but one who continually grows and develops.

The Disappearance of "Disciple" in the New Testament

Even though the term "disciple" is used almost 270 times in the New Testament, all of the occurrences are in the Gospels and the book of Acts. After Acts 21:16, the word "disciple" disappears and is never mentioned again. It's what disciple-maker Mike Breen calls "The Great Disappearance." Why did the word drop off? Did it become irrelevant or insignificant? Or could it be that there was another reason — possibly a cultural one?

Followers of Jesus were called disciples, a term rooted in the popular rabbinic relationship that was central to Jewish culture. The concept of the rabbi/disciple relationship was as common as a professor/student in our modern educational system. However, Greeks and Romans were oblivious to the concept. Mike Breen comments on the ambiguity:

> The Gospel was moving from Israel — from Jerusalem, Judea, and Samaria — and was now reaching the ends of the earth. In Corinth, there were very few (if any) rabbis and disciples. And the vast majority of the pagan cities such as Corinth, Ephesus, Alexandria, and Rome had no understanding of what the word 'disciple' meant because that word was always used in reference to a Jewish rabbi.[7]

Paul, writing to a predominately Roman and Greek audience, chose to simplify the concept by using a metaphor these non-Jews understood. He chose the familial relationship of a parent to a child. This paternalistic relationship of maturity, formation, and development is seen in almost every book of the New Testament. Children grow through both instruction from and imitation of their parents. In the same way, a disciple is expected to not only listen and implement what is heard, but to apply what is modeled in front of them.

Notice how many times Paul speaks to his disciples as "true sons" in the faith (Titus 1:4; 1 Timothy 1:2; and 2 Timothy 1:2). He consistently refers to believers in a paternalistic sense in his letters (1 Corinthians 4:14; Galatians 4:19; Ephesians 5:8; and 1 Thessalonians 5:5). John also calls believers "little children" in his epistles (1 John 2:1, 12, 13, 18, 28; 3:7, 18; 4:4; and 5:21). The clearest example is seen in 3 John 4: "I have no greater joy than this: to hear that my children [or disciples] are walking in the truth."

Rather than disappearing after the book of Acts, discipleship morphs into a slightly different image to communicate more clearly to people unfamiliar with the Jewish concept. This is not to say that Paul was wrong, just that we need to recover a full understanding of what Paul is saying by looking to the portrait of Jesus and His disciples in the Gospels. Ultimately, a true disciple of Christ is one who follows Jesus. Before you are able to go with the method of discipleship, you must have an intimate relationship with the Man behind the mission.

Of all the avenues for spreading the greatest message in the world — the redemption of humankind through His sacrifice — Jesus chose to spread it through twelve men and their future followers. Ultimately, through the passing of the centuries, the gospel has been entrusted to us. Should we not live with the same urgency with which Jesus and the twelve lived?

Every believer should be able to answer two questions: "Who am I discipling?" and "Who is discipling me?"

And every church should be able to answer two questions as well: "Do we have a comprehensive plan for making disciples?" and "Is our plan for disciple-making working?"

PART II

The Method of Making Disciples

CHAPTER 8

Making Disciples in a McChristian Culture

WE LIVE IN AN "I want it NOW!" society. Yet rarely can you actually get anything immediately and instantaneously. Amazon came up with a solution to this dilemma in 2005 when they implemented a two-day shipping option for a minimal yearly fee. Though the two-day wait is still not immediate, it's better than waiting a week. And for many people, it's a small price to pay to avoid leaving the comfort of your home, searching through endless store aisles, and standing in long lines to obtain that irresistible item on your "got-to-have-it" list.

Still, as the years have passed, two days has become two days too long, or perhaps we should say 47 hours and 30 minutes, to be more exact. In 2014, Amazon took their shipping strategy to the stratosphere, literally. They envisioned a day in the not-too-distant future when buyers will no longer have to wait days for a package to arrive. With a click of a button, an unmanned aerial vehicle can be dispatched to deliver a package to your doorstep in thirty minutes or less. The company boasts that Amazon Prime Air, as it is called, will one day revolutionize e-commerce as we know it.

The contraption they promoted looks like something out of a Star Trek episode, but the concept is not new. And as a sign of our times, it embodies our Western impatience. For most of us, "wait" is a four-letter word that wreaks havoc on our day. Everything in our lives revolves around immediacy, around doing things faster and getting results more quickly.

Whether you want a burger and fries or a frozen dinner, you can have it your way in roughly five minutes. This sense of urgency is not limited to food, either. For example, banking transactions — deposits, withdrawals, check cashing, and bill paying (yes, even your mortgage) — [1]can happen from the comfort of your bed with a device you can hold in your hand. You don't even have to change out of your pajamas. DVR boxes have revolutionized how we watch TV at night by eliminating time wasted by commercials. Each year, cell phones are replaced with a newer model to access faster download speeds and lightning fast processors. Our Amazon accounts are linked with Prime, iTunes has our credit card info on file for immediate downloads, and Little Caesar's always has our pizza "Hot-N-Ready."

Drive-Thru Christianity

We live in a world where everyone is in a hurry, but they are heading nowhere fast. Why the hurry? We're products of our cultural values. And you can either make a conscious effort to go against the grain or you will be swept away with the tide. Carrie Fisher fairly summed up our societal values when she observed, "Instant gratification takes too long."[2]

Sadly, this "have-it-now" mentality has spread like a virus, making its mark on not just the West, but through our cultural exports, on the rest of the world as well. This need for speed has infected not only the secular aspects of our lives but also our spiritual life. And this has not been good for the process of spiritual maturity. It should not surprise us that a mature Christian cannot be mass-produced through a quick and immediate process. The mass-production mindset of McChristianity is adversarial to discipleship and spiritual growth. Why? Because *you can't microwave disciples*. Discipleship is a Crock-Pot recipe.

When we implement "have-it-now" disciple-making models, we set the church up for unrealistic expectations. Discipleship takes time. You do not become a mature man or woman in the Christian faith overnight. "The besetting sin of the 21st century disciple is impatience," says Bill Hull, who after years of investing in others knows firsthand that you can't microwave a disciple.[3]

And that may be why so few people are actually discipling.

Squash or Oak Tree

In his helpful little book *The Green Letters*, Miles Stanford wrote these words: "It seems that most believers have difficulty in realizing and facing up to the inexorable fact that God does not hurry in His development of our Christian life."[4] Later in his book, Stanford underscores the importance of patience:

> A student asked the president of his school whether he could not take a shorter course than the one prescribed. "Oh yes," replied the President, "but then it depends on what you want to be. When God wants to make an oak, He takes a hundred years, but when He wants to make a squash, He takes six months."[5]

Why does squash-like growth entice us? We are trained to crave instant gratification. We like to see immediate results. The wait is short and the payoff is quick. But the God we serve is never in a rush to do anything. In fact, the only time in Scripture where we see God in a hurry is in Luke 15 when the prodigal son comes home and the father (God) runs to embrace his repentant son.

God is not in a rush to do his work. It took eleven years before Joseph was elevated to the right hand of the Pharaoh. Think about that. Eleven years. Without knowing the full story of Joseph's life from beginning to end, it would be natural to question the wisdom of God's timing in this situation. But God had work to do, work that took time. God had to press Joseph, mold him, and shape him for eleven years before he was ready to stand before Pharaoh.

God's timing is best. And there are qualities of godly character such as patience, perseverance, and endurance that can only be formed through waiting upon the Lord. Life is often like a puzzle. We all have a handful of pieces, but someone has taken the box with the picture on the cover. We are left wondering what the pieces fit together to form. After many years we pick up several more pieces, and pieces that once were disconnected begin to fit into place. In some cases, an image begins to take shape. And often, as we look back over decades and centuries, we realize that no pieces were ever wasted. Everything God gives us fits into the picture he has painted for our lives.

God uses every pressure, circumstance, and situation to shape and mold us into the person he desires us to be. Often his choice instrument for doing this is pain. Pain reveals areas in our lives that need to be formed. In the crucible of adversity, character is forged. Consider these examples of patience set by some of the founders of our faith:

- Noah endured mocking and humiliation for 90+ years while he constructed the Ark.
- Abraham waited for 30 years before God came through on his covenantal promise.
- Joseph endured isolation in a pit and incarceration in a prison before realizing the promise God made to him 11 years before.
- Moses wandered in the wilderness for four decades waiting to enter the land that was promised.
- Jesus waited 30 years according to the plan and wisdom of God before he began his earthly ministry.

Each of these men learned to wait upon the Lord, to trust in God's lead and his plans. Could it be that one of the reasons we are not seeing more intentional discipleship take place today is that we do not want to wait upon the Lord, that we lack the patience to persevere in the long-term commitment required to make disciples? Filling empty seats can be fixed in a few weeks. Discipling new Christians into mature followers of Jesus can take a lifetime. So where do you begin? Well, for starters, begin with the Bible.

A Walk to Remember

Before I ever met her, Kandi (now my wife) was actively involved in discipling women. Her love for the Old Testament was infectious to the ladies who met with her in her discipleship group. And she continues to pursue her love for discipling women today. With four discipleship groups running simultaneously between the two of us, our home is constantly filled with conversations and stories of challenges and victories as we study the Bible and apply it to our lives. Recently Kandi shared with me a four-step process she has seen God use to grow believers in her groups in understanding of the Bible. The steps are Remember, Reflect, Retell, and Repeat.

We all begin by reading the Scriptures, but so often we end there. We may answer a few questions, but we rarely come back to the Bible to dig into it again. Remembering what you already know is as important, or more, than introducing new information. As we see in the Bible, God consistently reminds the Israelites to remember — especially to remember what he has done for them.

> Then Moses said to the people, "Remember this day when you came out of Egypt, out of the place of slavery, for the LORD brought you out of here by the strength of His hand. Nothing leavened may be eaten" (Ex. 13:3).
>
> "Remember the Sabbath day" (Ex. 20:8).
>
> "Remember that you were a slave in the land of Egypt, and the LORD your God brought you out of there with a strong hand and an outstretched arm. That is why the LORD your God has commanded you to keep the Sabbath day" (Deut. 5:15).
>
> "Remember what Moses the LORD's servant commanded you when he said, 'The LORD your God will give you rest, and He will give you this land'" (Josh. 1:13).

Why do we remember? Because intentional remembering leads us to reflection. God envisioned the Sabbath to be a scheduled event as much as a state of mind, a chance to reflect on his goodness and grace over the previous week. Reflection means meditating on God's precepts. Memorize his commands. Enjoy his presence. Savor his blessings.

Reflection leads to retelling. God knows that we are forgetful, so he created a system to reduce our lapses of memory, particularly pertaining to his work in our lives. Standing at the banks of the Jordan, the people of Israel were eager to enter the Promised Land. One obstacle stood in their way — deep, rushing water. Instantly, when the priests' feet touched the water, the stream backed up. It was as if someone had turned off a faucet somewhere upstream. Consequently, the nation of Israel (somewhere between a half-million to two million people) followed the priests across the dry river bed. As soon as they crossed, water resumed flowing. God kept his promise to lead them into the Promised Land, and He did so in a miraculous manner.

After crossing the Jordan, the Israelites were instructed to appoint twelve men, each representing one of the twelve tribes of Israel, to build a rock pile. The reason?

> "That this will be a sign among you. When your children ask in time to come, 'What do those stones mean to you?' then you shall tell them that the waters of the Jordan were cut off before the ark of the covenant of the LORD. When it passed over the Jordan, the waters of the Jordan were cut off. So these stones shall be to the people of Israel a memorial forever" (Josh. 4:6–7 ESV).

In a day without journals, computers, or tablets (iPads, not stone tablets), God, through a pile of rocks, imprinted his supernatural intervention upon their minds. "Don't ever forget what I did for you," the Lord said. "My faithfulness among you will be retold for generations to come."

Throughout the book of Joshua, God continued to work supernaturally, prompting the people to erect stone memorials seven times.[6] Today, while we may pray for God to work in our lives, how many of us actually keep a record of his faithfulness? These spiritual stones — records of God's faithfulness — fortify our faith during the difficult seasons of life. Again and again, they become platforms for praise. Forgetting God's goodness is not an option in his kingdom.

But the process is not complete until it is repeated or shared with someone. I instruct my discipleship groups to share with someone what they read during their time in the Word. Tell your spouse, tell your friends, tell your family, and most importantly, tell your children. Rabbis knew that repetition was the mother of learning. A rabbi once said, "A person who repeats his lesson a 100 times is not as good as one who repeats his lesson 101."[7] God may be the father of truth, but repetition is the mother of all learning.

Jews recite the Shema — the portion of Scripture we know as Deuteronomy 6:4–9 — daily. In the Shema God embedded a special word of instruction of discipleship to parents:

> "Listen, Israel: The LORD our God, the LORD is One. Love the LORD your God with all your heart, with all your soul, and with all your strength. These words that I am giving you today are to be in your heart. *Repeat them to your children.* Talk about them when you sit in your house and when you walk along the road, when you lie down and when you get up. Bind them as a sign on your hand and let them be a symbol on your forehead. Write them on the doorposts of your house and on your gates" (my emphasis).

Notice that in this passage *all* of the elements are included: Remember, Reflect, Retell, and Repeat.

Slow Down

In addition to these suggestions for getting people involved in studying the Bible, here are three guidelines that can help you remain on the challenging path of discipleship over the long haul. First and most importantly, *set reasonable goals.* Jesus invested *three years* with his disciples before he commissioned them to go to the nations. Don't expect a forty-day study or a twelve-week class to immediately produce mature disciples. Consider investing a minimum of twelve-to-eighteen months into your discipleship group.

A few years ago I was invited to join several other leaders in a cabin at the base of Signal Mountain, Tennessee, on a cold Saturday morning to formulate a strategy to disciple the men of Chattanooga. The enthusiasm in the room was palpable, with many of the men expressing their desire to disciple other men.

The moderator posed a question to the entire group: "What are we going to do now?" Without hesitation, one man shot his hand up and spoke before he was called on, "Let's set a goal to find five hundred disciple-makers by the end of the year."

"Amens" were muttered throughout the room. To this point, I had remained quiet. First, I was the youngest man in the room; second, I was the newest pastor in town. But at this I sheepishly raised my hand. "Robby," called the man in front. "You haven't said much. What are your thoughts?"

"I know I'm the new guy here," I said, "but I think we may be starting with the wrong metric in mind. Instead of setting a goal to locate *five hundred* disciple-makers in our city, let's run the magnet through the sand to discover who is actually a disciple-maker first. We may only locate five men who are ready to invest their lives into the lives of others." After that, I was invited to join a smaller group of five men with the purpose of pulling together a disciple-making strategy — one with reasonable goals.[8]

Secondly, *start a discipleship group.* I know that seems obvious, but at some point you actually need to get started. You can begin investing today. If you are a man, find a group of men to disciple. If you are a woman, gather several women together. It's challenging to take someone on a journey you have never been on yourself, but it's not impossible. *You don't need another Bible study to get ready for this.* Take the Bible you already know and study it with two or three other people weekly.

Addition vs. Multiplication

Steve Murrell, missionary, disciple-maker, and author, shared his philosophy of discipleship with me over a lunch of sushi in Nashville several years ago. I had just read his book *WikiChurch* (in a single day — I couldn't put it down!), and I had sent him a tweet asking if he visited the States and would be open to meeting. He graciously accepted my invitation, and the door was opened for our lunch meeting.

Steve shared with me how in 1984, he and his wife, Deborah, went to the Philippines for a one-month summer mission trip. He joked that the one-month trip had been extended for thirty years. Victory Manila, the church he eventually planted, has now grown to fifteen satellite locations with forty-eight preaching pastors ministering to almost 60,000 people. Eight thousand discipleship groups meet in coffee shops, offices, dormitories, parks, and homes and on the steps outside the church on Sunday mornings and throughout the week.

I asked Steve to explain his system for developing so many leaders to facilitate that large number of groups. He chuckled and replied,

> We have a training system for those interested in discipling others. But it's impossible to manage. The organic nature of group formation forces us to release control. We are sometimes forced to enlist newer Christians to disciple new believers. "How much of the New Testament have you read?" is a question we ask those interested in facilitating a group. Some tell us, "I just finished the book of Matthew." To that we say: "Good — you can lead. This man hasn't read *any* of the Bible. You are a whole book ahead of him."

I realize that some church leaders aren't comfortable placing new believers in a position of leadership. But I think Steve highlights an important point. One of the reasons we are not seeing discipleship take place in churches is because *church leadership may assume that it needs to execute the ministry instead of empowering others to do it.* (Remember when we looked at Ephesians 4:11 – 13?) I'll admit that I personally have a tendency to wait for believers to mature before allowing them to serve in ministry, but we need to balance our caution here with the understanding that ministry is the pathway to maturity, not vice versa. Empowering others to do the work of ministry requires trust, but it's essential that we find a balance that equalizes the swinging of the pendulum from the extremes of waiting too long and not waiting long enough.

So here is where we need to sense the need for balance. We cannot do all the work, so we need to release and empower others.

At the same time, we aren't in a rush to get this done. So slow down. This is a marathon, not a sprint. Conserve your energy and plan for the future. Richard Foster has said, "Our tendency is to overestimate what we can accomplish in one year, but underestimate what we can accomplish in ten years."[9]

Discipleship takes time, so we need to plan on dedicating that time and waiting on the results, which can be mind-blowing when we understand the power of multiplication (more on that in the next chapter). Just remember, you cannot microwave disciples. It's a Crock-Pot recipe. And it takes time for maturity to take root. The wait is long, but the results are worth it.

CHAPTER 9

One for All, Not One at a Time

AFTER CHURCH ON A HOT, humid August day in New Orleans, my pastor, David Platt, approached me to ask me a question. At this point, I had been a believer for nine months. Two months earlier, a friend from college had suggested that I seek out a discipleship group. Coming from a Roman Catholic background, I had no idea what she was talking about at first. "Do people disciple others in the church?" I asked. The concept was foreign to me. But I promised her I would pray about it.

I did. I devoted myself to praying that God would send someone into my life to teach me how to follow Jesus. David, after church one Sunday, had a question for me: "Would you be interested in meeting once a week to study the Bible, memorize Scripture, and pray together?" It was the answer to my prayer.

We began meeting once a week. Our routine was always the same. I would pick him up just before lunch at the seminary where he taught and then drop him off again just before his Ph.D. Seminar at 1:30. We would eat General Tso's Chicken, pizzas, or just grab some coffee and then discuss Scripture, missions, and how to put it all into practice. Our weekly appointments continued for five months. At that point we decided to enlarge the group to include a few other guys, since I had decided to pursue seminary education.

Those one-on-one meetings worked great for that season of my life. David was an amazing teacher, patient with this young convert whom some had labeled "ignorance on fire." There was a reason for that label. I didn't know *much* about Christ, but what I did know I was fanatical about. I immediately set out to duplicate with someone else everything I was learning from our meetings. I shared the gospel with a guy named Casey, a personal trainer at the gym where I trained, and he accepted, to my surprise, the invitation to place his trust in Christ. He was radically saved.

So now what? What do you do with a person who has just been born again?

Hit the repeat button!

I had my first disciple, even though I still needed to be discipled. But I had noticed early in the discipleship process that you never quite feel confident enough to invest in another person. You just do it, out of obedience to Jesus. Even the disciples, gazing in the sky at Jesus' departure, needed some prodding from the angels to get out and do what Jesus had asked them to do. Those you disciple will need your encouragement and support.

While there are some benefits to meeting one-on-one with someone, there are also many limitations. These limitations were evident early on in my initial meetings with Casey. So just as my own discipleship group had widened to include a few other men, Casey and I opened up our group to some others. It made all the difference.

Don't ignore this point as something minor or irrelevant: *Group size matters*. It mattered to Jesus as well. In addition to having a clear system for making disciples, Jesus wisely utilized differently sized groups on the pathway to growth. We can roughly categorize them into five different types: the *crowd*, the *congregation*, the *community*, the *core*, and finally, his *close* relationships.

The Crowd

From the very beginning of his earthly ministry, crowds surrounded Jesus. From the early hours of the morning to late at night, they sought him out. Mark tells us of a time when Jesus was praying early one morning, and Peter approached him to say that the multitudes were seeking him.

> Very early in the morning, while it was still dark, He got up, went out, and made His way to a deserted place. And He was praying there. Simon and his companions went searching for

Him. They found Him and said, "Everyone's looking for You!" (Mark 1:35–37).

And this wasn't just a few people. As Peter said, "everyone" was asking for him. Jesus' response strikes our ears today as rather peculiar: "And He said to them, 'Let's go on to the neighboring villages so that I may preach there too. This is why I have come'" (Mark 1:38).

Jesus, unlike many occupied with numbers, wasn't primarily concerned about drawing a crowd for the sake of counting heads. He was focused on doing the Father's will, something deeper and greater than temporary success and worldly acclaim.

The Congregation

Luke 10:1 tells us that Jesus "appointed 70 [or 72] others [disciples], and He sent them ahead of Him in pairs to every town and place where He Himself was about to go" to heal the sick and proclaim the advent of the kingdom. This committed band of disciples was empowered as evangelists to bear witness to the coming kingdom of God. Later, just prior to Jesus' ascension to the Father, a group of 120 believers professed faith in him (Acts 1). They were instructed to wait for the coming Holy Spirit on Pentecost.[1]

This group, smaller than the crowds, was composed of those who identified as followers of Jesus. They were serious about following him, but they weren't always with Jesus as he traveled. I refer to this larger group of 70 to 150 as the "congregation." Today this would be roughly synonymous with membership in a local church. After Jesus' resurrection and ascension, the 120 men and women mentioned here made up the membership roll of the early church.

The Community

Jesus had a smaller group of twelve men whom he called out to leave their families, friends, and careers to follow him. He invested the majority of his ministry into mentoring this group of disciples. Author and pastor Eugene Peterson has said, "Jesus, it must be remembered, restricted nine-tenths of His ministry to twelve Jews."[2] The lion's share of his time was devoted to this "small group" and not to the crowds or the congregation. The purpose of this group was fellowship and community.

Don't Leave Disciple-Making to Chance

Discipleship is a process. Have you ever wondered why Jesus waited 33 years to go to the cross? He could have simply marched toward Jerusalem, claimed that he was God, ticked off the leaders, and been killed. The execution of would-be messiahs leading insurrections against the government was commonplace.[3] But Jesus didn't do that. Instead, he invested in a group of disciples for three years. Much of what we know about Jesus comes from these firsthand accounts of his life. Jesus came to die for our sins, yes, but key to his larger mission of saving the world was the selecting, investing in, and sending out these twelve men.[4]

Why does this matter? Because in church ministry it is easy to focus on the goal and to forget about the means to achieve it. If our goal is to change lives and to reach the world with the message of the gospel, we need to consider the best way to do that. I would argue that we need to recover a healthy and biblical understanding of small groups.

Are small groups indispensable for life change? Ed Stetzer and Eric Geiger think so. In their book *Transformational Groups* they provide evidence to support the indispensability of meeting in a smaller context. The findings revealed that people in a group read the Bible more attentively, pray more regularly, confess sins more frequently, share the gospel more freely, give more generously, and serve more faithfully than those by themselves.[5] Discipleship, according to Stetzer and Geiger, cannot happen *outside* of a community. They write,

The two are inseparable, and this must be communicated clearly and consistently by leadership. If you wonder why the people lack any sense of investment in community, it may be because the leaders lack it as well. When the pastor sends the wrong message, you should not be surprised when it results in the wrong outcome.[6]

Leaders should lead by example, a truth foundational in the Master's model of discipleship.

The Core

Even though the majority of his time was spent with the twelve disciples, there are also several times recorded in the Gospels when Jesus took three disciples with him for intensive times of equipping: Peter, James, and John. There are at least five times where we see this happening in the Gospels:

- At the healing of Peter's mother-in-law (Mark 1:29)
- At the raising of Jairus' daughter from the dead (Mark 5:37)
- On the mount of transfiguration with Jesus (Mark 9:2)
- At the Olivet Discourse, when Jesus explained end-time events (Mark 13:3)
- With Jesus in the Garden of Gethsemane, just prior to his trial and crucifixion (Matt. 26:37)

These three men were privy to intimate times of encouragement, edification, and education. We can only assume why Jesus regularly retreated with these men while the others were left behind. Matthew Henry in his commentary on 1 John 2:12–14 said, "All Christians are not of the same standing and stature; there are babes in Christ, there are grown men, and old disciples."[7] Jesus probably identified their readiness to receive the implanted truths he was sharing. Regardless, each of them served the Lord faithfully until their deaths.

Close Relationships

Even though the Bible records Jesus ministering to a variety of individuals at different stages of his ministry, we never see any evidence that Jesus engaged in an ongoing one-on-one discipling relationship with anyone. Jesus met with individuals like Nicodemus (John 3) and the woman at the well (John 4), but these were isolated, occasional meetings, not what we would call intimate friendships. The Bible highlights that Jesus had an intimate relationship with John and Peter, as we see in his restoration of Peter on the shore of the Sea of Galilee (John 21). But the Gospels also let us know that Jesus discipled Peter, James, and John as a group — not as individuals, one-on-one.

This does not mean that one-on-one discipling is unbiblical or ineffective. But it does suggest that there are advantages to discipleship in a community with others. I always tell people that if you have a choice, meet with two or three other people instead of meeting one-on-one. What's wrong with the one-on-one mentoring relationship? Didn't Jesus pair his disciples up two-by-two as they went out in ministry?

Yes, he did, and there are certainly times when this is appropriate. But here is where the wisdom of Solomon applies: "Two are better than one.... And though a man might prevail against one who is alone, two will withstand him — a threefold cord is not quickly broken" (Eccl. 4:9, 12 ESV). Two are good, but three are better, according to history's wisest man.

Growth Happens in Groups

Mathetes, the word most commonly translated as "disciple" in the New Testament, is used 239 times in the plural form in the Gospels and the book of Acts. That same word is used only twenty-five times in the singular form. And out of those twenty-five occurrences, twenty of them are references to John as the "disciple" whom Jesus loved or speak generally of a nameless "disciple." There is only one time in the entire Bible when the singular word *disciple* is used to describe an individual, a reference to Joseph of Arimathea. The disciples of Jesus understood that discipleship happens in community, as a group. As one historian has noted,

> "As presented in the Gospels, discipleship involves not just an individualistic relationship of a single pupil to his teacher but the formation of a group around the teacher who has called the group into existence.[8]

Again, I'm not trying to be that guy who opposes one-on-one discipleship. We need to be flexible and attentive to the context and God's leading, and there are times and seasons that call for a break from the group approach. Perhaps you need to address a particular issue with someone in a season of struggle. I meet with individuals for personal discipleship, but it's always in addition to participation in the group, never in place of it.

I found a great reminder of this reading about the Muir Woods just north of San Francisco. The Muir Woods are an incredible forest of breathtakingly large sequoia trees. These trees, reaching almost 250 feet into the sky, are said to be the largest living things on earth. Many of them have been alive for more than 1,500 years, and they have endured nature's fiercest winds and storms.

What is the secret to their longevity? You might assume that they have deep roots that grow for hundreds of feet into the soil and anchor them to the ground. But you would be wrong. The roots of these large sequoias only descend a mere four feet into the earth — extremely shallow for such colossal trees. Instead, "the reason for the sequoias' sustained growth is their support system beneath the earth's surface. Sequoia trees only grow in rows or groves. You will never find them growing alone. The roots of these trees interlock with each other, and this is the secret to their survival through the centuries."[9]

This is a lesson for us, as the body of Christ. No sequoia grows alone. Neither does a disciple of Jesus.

Paul's Preferred Group Size

Now, some of you may be following this and object at this point. "But what about Paul? Didn't Paul disciple one-on-one?" What about his remarks to Timothy in his final letter? In 2 Timothy 2:1–2 we read, "You then, my child, be strengthened by the grace that is in Christ Jesus, and what *you have heard from me* in the presence of many *witnesses* entrust to faithful men who will be able to teach others also" (ESV, emphasis mine). The key word in verse 2 is *witnesses*.

Strong's concordance tells us that the word *martus* can describe someone who has "information or knowledge of something and hence, one who can give information, bring to light, or confirm something."[10] And it's the same word used in Acts 1:8:

"But you will receive power when the Holy Spirit has come on you, and you will be My *witnesses* in Jerusalem, in all Judea and Samaria, and to the ends of the earth" (emphasis mine). It is synonymous with the word *believer* or *disciple*. In fact, read Acts 1:8 again and make a substitution: "But you will receive power when the Holy Spirit has come on you, and you will be My *disciples* in Jerusalem, in all Judea and Samaria, and to the ends of the earth." So what does this have to do with 2 Timothy 2:2?

For years, I interpreted the word *witnesses* as simple bystanders, "yes men" who validated Paul's message. But Timothy didn't need anyone to authenticate Paul's message. At this point he had known Paul for fifteen years. Instead, I think Paul is reminding Timothy of Paul's teaching in community, to the crowd and to smaller groups. Note that Paul uses plural nouns in his formula for making disciples: "What you have heard from me in the presence of *many witnesses* [plural], entrust to faithful *men* [plural] who will be able to teach *others* [plural]" (ESV, emphasis mine). Paul understood the importance of multiplication.

Finally, Paul rarely traveled by himself. Whenever he had a choice, he would set out with several other co-workers, men like Barnabas, Silas, John Mark, Timothy, Titus, or Luke. Obviously, there were advantages to traveling in a group. Paul could draw from the strength of his mission partners as he stood toe-to-toe with political and religious leaders. Additionally, his companions could multiply his efforts by going ahead of him to prepare for his arrival or, after he had left, remaining behind to help organize new believers.

We can also safely assume that Paul used his missionary journeys as a platform for discipling his traveling buddies. These travel companions formed an itinerant discipleship group, and like Christ, Paul did much of his discipleship in a group setting.

Eight Reasons to Disciple in a Group

Hopefully, I have convinced you of biblical reasons to disciple believers in a D-Group. Before we wrap up, I would like to offer eight reasons why you should consider group-based discipleship.

Again, I want to be clear: The Bible never prescribes a particular model for discipling others, and as we have seen, Jesus invested in groups of varying sizes. Larger groups learned from his teachings and miracles, while his closest followers benefited from personal discipleship and specific instruction. While one-on-one discipling is valid and has its purposes, I want you to seriously consider eight reasons why it makes sense to meet in a D-Group of three to five instead of privately with one person.

1. Avoid the ping-pong match.

With two people, one of you is clearly the leader and the other is the learner. As the leader, you are responsible to keep the ball in play. "Mike, how was your day?" "Good," responds Mike. You probe deeper by asking, "Any insights from your Scripture reading this week?" "I enjoyed it," Mike briefly replies. Your conversation will progress as far as you can engage the person you are mentoring. When others join you, the pressure to lead is lessened as others share their insights and ask questions.

2. One-on-one is difficult to reproduce.

This is one of the primary reasons why I don't advocate a one-on-one model. This model can be challenging to reproduce because the person in whom you are investing has a tendency to look at you much the way Timothy looked at the apostle Paul. Mentees, after a year or two in a discipling relationship, have said to me, "I could never do with another person what you did with me." They assume that they need to have several decades of walking with Jesus under their belt and possibly a seminary education. By contrast, a group takes a journey together. And as the discipleship journey unfolds over the course of a year, Mike will think to himself, "I may not be like Robby, but if Bubba can do this and Ralph can do this, maybe I can as well."

Moreover, in my experience most group members will not *feel* ready to begin their own groups. Neither did the disciples, but Jesus didn't make it optional. Remember, the discipling relationship has a goal, and that goal is not achieved until the mentee actually becomes a mentor to someone else. The player should become a coach. I recall a local discipleship ministry that uses a one-on-one approach lamenting about its minimal reproduction rate of 25 to 30 percent. One of the reasons for this low rate, according to the ministry leader, is the difficulty they have in convincing those they mentor that they can lead others.

3. A group of two tends to become a counseling session.

Many people are familiar with counseling, and some churches adopt a therapeutic model in their small groups. While there is certainly a place for counseling, I don't believe that a discipleship relationship should be a counseling session. With a group of two this is difficult to avoid, and some have shared with me that they spend the majority of their time in one-on-one discipling solving personal problems. Again, there is a place for applying biblical wisdom to personal life issues, but a pattern of dispensing therapeutic advice every week should not define the group.

4. A group of three to five has built-in accountability.

In the first D-Group I led, two of the three men involved came prepared with a Bible-reading journal I had asked them to complete. One of the men had failed to make any entries. Prior to joining the D-Group, he had lots of excuses for not reading the Bible. "It's difficult for me to understand," he told me. Seeing that the other two men had done their entries, I said to him, "Can you just try journaling for the next five days? Right now, you have no evidence to prove that it doesn't work. Try it and tell us next time if it works for you or not."

The next week, he arrived with a smile on his face: "I can't wait to share what I heard from God through his Word this week." Seeing the excitement of the others in the group challenged him to contribute to the group and to his own spiritual development. A group of three to five provides a built-in accountability system.

5. A multiplication strategy is exponentially faster than an addition strategy.

Discipleship in small groups can easily translate to exponential growth. I realize that this is difficult for people to grasp in the short term. It's hard to look at the work of an evangelist who is speaking to hundreds, if not thousands, of people and compare his results to the work someone does in a small group discipling three people a year.

That's because we rarely think long-term. Consider a hypothetical situation to grasp the long-term effectiveness of exponential growth. In this example we will pit a slow-moving disciple-maker against a hard-working, road-traveling evangelist. Let's assume that our disciple-maker in his first year reaches three people, investing deeply into their lives. In that same year, the evangelist reaches a thousand people, mostly through one-to-two-day preaching meetings at churches. In the second year, the disciple-maker equips his group of three to go out and form their own group of four (himself plus three others). The evangelist continues his work of preaching and reaches another thousand. At this point, the disciple-maker has reached nine people, while the evangelist has reached two thousand.

As you may have guessed, those numbers will radically change with the passing of time. In the next year, as the second generation groups split up and form new groups, the disciple-maker's influence will spread to twenty-seven. In the following year, it will hit 243, then 2,187. The next, 19,683. After six years, the disciple-maker's influence has reached over 19,000 people. The evangelist has had a steady pattern of reaching a total of 6,000.[11]

These are just the numbers of one disciple-maker. If we add up every disciple-maker's influence in this process, every person on the planet would be reached multiple times over after thirty years. While this is obviously hypothetical and the fruit of ministry is ultimately dependent upon God's timing and the work of the Holy Spirit, we cannot ignore the potential that is unlocked by shifting our strategy from addition to multiplication. As pastors and church leaders begin to grasp this concept, our churches can begin to reposition into mission-training stations, rather than clubs where discipleship is optional. Discipleship must be *the* ministry of the church and not *a* ministry of the church for a world-changing movement to emerge.

6. A one-on-one group can be intimidating.

Have you ever sat across the table from someone and exposed the deep dark secrets of your life for ninety minutes? Have you ever tried to do that with one person, meeting weekly for an entire year? For many people, the thought of this makes their palms sweat. For men especially, the thought of meeting one-on-one for a long period of time may strike panic in their hearts, even more than the thought of speaking before a crowd of 300 people. Most people are more comfortable sharing in a group setting, and the inclusion of others diminishes the reluctance to commit on the front end. It's less intimidating.

7. You grow as a group.

We are fallible creatures. Even with the best theological education, we can be led astray. Thus, I believe that the Bible was meant to be studied in a group setting. When there are others studying with us, it guards against teaching something unbiblical. No true believer willingly teaches heresy, but often there is genuine confusion or misunderstanding. With a larger group, you have the advantage of additional people who can broaden the understanding and perspective of the entire group. In addition, questions posed by group members can take the conversation to places a single facilitator might never consider. I have found that I've grown in my own understanding as I've grown together with other believers.

8. Jesus discipled in groups.

I know that I risk being a broken record here, but it bears repeating once more. If we are called to be followers of Christ, should we not also copy his methods? Jesus preached to the multitudes on a few occasions, but the majority of his time was poured into a small group. Why not follow in his footsteps and do what Jesus did? The Babylonian Talmud, a commentary on the Old Testament, affirms the importance of learning — even as a teacher discipling others — in a group: "Much have I learned from my teachers, even more from my haverim [community], but from my disciples, most of all."[12]

Don't Be Unprepared

I know of many pastors who are praying for revival in our country and around the world. Only God can breathe his breath of renewal upon us, and it is essential for us to pray and ask for him to do just that. But as we pray, we must also prepare. It is crucial that we are ready with a plan and a strategy to handle the revival when God pours out his Spirit on the church. Does your church have a system in place to respond if 3,000 people were to respond after a single evangelistic message? Do you have a prescriptive, repeatable, and effective process for spiritual growth?

What we learn from Jesus and Paul and the New Testament church is that they were ready. They knew their mission. They focused on the long-term goal. As they prayed, they prepared for the harvest that God would bring. Nothing in this world happens by chance, and God is sovereign in accomplishing his plans. Discipleship is no different. So let's be ready for the harvest when it comes. Begin today by planning for tomorrow.

CHAPTER 10

Roadblocks to Making Disciples

SEVERAL YEARS AGO OUR DISCIPLESHIP ministry set up a booth at a denominational convention. Tim, our disciple-making pastor, conducted an informal survey by asking fifty pastors if they had a comprehensive strategy for making disciples. Sadly, none of those he asked had one. A prominent pastor in the Southern Baptist Convention said to him, "We've collected all the data, but we still don't have a comprehensive strategy." Hearing this, Tim and I felt burdened to do something.

We knew that "comprehensive" did not have to mean "complicated." In fact, one of our goals was to keep things as simple as we could. Most churches are complex organisms, and one of the greatest challenges leaders face today is cutting through the programs and traditions to regain a simple focus on the essential mission of the church.

Albert Einstein once wrote, "Out of complexity, find simplicity." This quote was the inspiration for the book *Simple Church*. In it Thom Rainer and Eric Geiger present four elements that help churches to simplify to the essentials: *clarity, movement, alignment,* and *focus.* After extensive research, the authors developed these elements into a simple process that churches can follow. As I considered the need for a discipleship strategy, I realized that many of the same principles in this book could be applied to discipleship.

Clarity

Rainer and Geiger define clarity as "the ability of the process to be communicated and understood by the people.... If the process is not clearly defined so that everyone is speaking the same language, there is confusion and frustration."[1] One of the first things a church needs to do in establishing a plan for discipleship is to define what they are doing. According to Bill Hull, many churches throw "the word disciple around freely, but too often with no definition."[2] New Testament Professor Scot McKnight explains the danger of failing to define what you mean:

> If one understands discipleship as "daily routine," then one will produce those who have daily routines. If one understands discipleship as "evangelistic ministry," then one will produce evangelists. If one understands discipleship as "Bible study," then one will produce biblical scholars. If one understands discipleship as "effective operations," then one will produce administrative geniuses.[3]

A quick survey of the Christian landscape will uncover several definitions of discipleship. Each is worth considering, as they all emphasize different elements of the discipleship task. Fortunately, Jesus, in His infinite wisdom, did not prescribe for us a single *model* of how to disciple. Instead, He gave us a *mandate*: Make disciples! He didn't give us a single *process*; he left us with several *principles* and showed us by His own examples.

Personally, I have found Robert Coleman's book *The Master Plan of Evangelism* to be one of the most helpful resources in understanding the timeless principles we find in the example of Jesus. Jesus left things like the group's size, its length, and its particularities up to the disciple-maker. And we need to avoid being too dogmatic where Jesus gives us latitude. But with much freedom comes much responsibility. Rather than using your freedom as a license for laziness, decide on the system that works best in your church context and then faithfully follow it.

Are We Speaking the Same Language?

I often get asked the question: "What is discipleship?" Usually I answer it by explaining what discipleship is not.

It's not a Class.	*It's not a Quick Process.*
It's not a Seminar.	*It's not a Quick Fix.*
It's not a Degree you earn.	*It's not Reserved for Super*
It's not a Program.	*Christians.*
It's not a 12-Week Bible Study.	*It's not Hard.*
It's not a 40-Day Home Group.	*It's not an Option!*

Okay. That's what discipleship is not. So here is what I tell people it is.

Discipleship is *intentionally equipping believers with the Word of God through accountable relationships empowered by the Holy Spirit in order to replicate faithful followers of Christ.* When people become disciples, they learn what Jesus said and live out what Jesus did (Matt. 28:19–20).

Keep in mind that every process you develop must be *contextualized.* A "one size fits all" approach will not work. Discipleship in Chattanooga is very different from discipleship in San Francisco or the Dominican Republic. After preaching an evangelistic crusade, D. L. Moody was met after the service by a man who disapproved of his evangelistic strategy. Moody responded by asking a question, "It's evident that you don't agree with my evangelism method. What's your evangelistic model for winning the lost?" The man replied, "I don't have a particular method." Moody quickly replied: "I think I'll stick with mine."

Study, read, and then decide what works best for your church. But regardless of which model, material, or manner you affirm, decide on a plan and *stick with it.* Be clear about your definitions and your process if you want to have a simple plan.

Movement

The home I grew up in backed up to a wooded area. Tall tales of monsters and evil men residing deep within the dark woods circulated throughout our neighborhood. As a child, I never ventured into the woods unless I had an adult with me.

Every Easter my father, grandfather, uncle, and I, with walking sticks in hand, would embark on an adventure into the forest. The dense underbrush coupled with towering trees created an eerie atmosphere. At first, we would aggressively prune shrubs and step on branches to create a path, but once we made it into the heart of the forest, we discovered a large expanse of paths and trails. When we went out there one Easter, I discovered an opening that led me back home — or so I thought.

Focused on the task at hand, I wasn't aware that I had wandered off and was now walking alone.

"Dad!" I cried out in fear, "Where are you?"

"Johnny. Paw Paw!" I screamed, "Are you here?"

As I was frantically looking around, my family was nowhere to be found. Terrified, I did what any seven-year-old would do. I cried. Soon my father appeared from a nearby brush. He grabbed me and led me on a new path out of the woods.

I learned something that day that I haven't forgotten. *It's difficult to lead when you don't know where you are going.* You can't take someone on a journey you've never been on. My dad knew the woods; I didn't. And I needed him to help me get out.

Many believers — sadly, even many pastors — have never had the privilege of being discipled by another person. Mike Breen, leader of *3D Ministries*, a movement that emphasizes biblical discipleship and planting missional churches, highlights this problem:

> Maybe you've grown up in church. Maybe you've even gone to seminary. Maybe you lead a church, small group or Bible study. Maybe you've read every Christian book there is to read from the last 50 years. Great! It means you have an outstanding informational foundation. But you still might need to be discipled in the way that the Bible understands discipleship."[4]

Could it be that believers minimize discipleship in the church because they never had the privilege of being discipled? That might be the first step you need to take as a leader. It is difficult — nearly impossible — to lead someone on a journey on which you have never been yourself.

Alignment

Jesus' command to make disciples was not a *theoretical* expectation. Not only did Jesus tells his disciples to disciple others, but he also showed them how to do it. Similarly, Paul sketches out the same roadmap in the final letter he writes to his spiritual son in the faith:

> You then, my child, be strengthened by the grace that is in Christ Jesus, and what you have heard from me in the presence of many witnesses entrust to faithful men who will be able to teach others also (2 Tim. 2:1–2 ESV).

This verse was one of the first verses of Scripture that Dawson Trotman, the founder of the Navigators, asked Billy Graham to memorize. Dr. Graham explained its importance to me:

> This is like a mathematical formula for spreading the gospel and enlarging the church. Paul taught Timothy. Timothy shared what he knew with faithful men. And the faithful men were supposed to teach others also. And so the process goes on. If every believer followed this pattern, the church could reach the entire world in one generation. If the church followed this pattern, we could reach the world in one generation. Mass crusades in which I believe and to which I have committed my life will never accomplish the Great Commission; one-on-one relationships will.[5]

A common misconception is that the ability to "make disciples" is a gift of the Spirit that only elite, super-Christians are expected to possess. But as we have seen in our study, all believers have been given authority to disciple by Christ (Matt. 28:18), and all Christians have been commanded to disciple others (Matt. 28:19–20)!

Before people will do what you ask, they will watch what you do. Pastors, you can't expect your people to do something you aren't doing. What group of men are you meeting with once a week for prayer? With whom are you studying the Scriptures? With whom and to whom are you holding yourselves accountable? A church member once said to me, "Your talk talks and your walk talks, but your walk talks louder than your talk talks." The way you live speaks volumes about the degree of disciple-making taking place in your church.

To borrow a quote commonly misattributed to the Indian states-man Mahatma Gandhi: "Be the change you wish to see in the world!" The men, women, and youth of your congregations look to you for guidance. Jesus stood as an example for the walks of Paul, Timothy, and all the brothers and sisters in him throughout the ages. Likewise, pastors are to be prime examples of disciplemakers. If you aren't seeing discipleship take place in your church, it may be because you aren't involved in discipling relationships.

The poet Edgar A. Guest said it well in "Sermons We See":

> I'd rather see a sermon,
> than hear one any day;
> I'd rather one should walk with me
> than merely tell the way.
> The eye's a better pupil
> and more willing than the ear;
> Fine counsel is confusing,
> but example's always clear.
> The best of all the preachers
> are the men who live their creeds.
> For to see good put in action
> is what everybody needs.
> I soon can learn to do it
> if you'll let me see it done.
> I can watch your hands in action,
> but your tongue too fast may run.
> The lecture you deliver
> may be very wise and true,
> But I'd rather get my lessons
> by observing what you do.
> For I might misunderstand you
> and the high advice you give,
> But there's no misunderstanding
> how you act and how you live.[6]

You can't change the path you've been on, but you can change where you're heading.

Focus

I have mixed emotions about all the hype surrounding discipleship right now. On the one hand, I'm grateful that people are talking. The dialogue thrills me. For the first time, people aren't looking at me with a confused look on their faces when I speak about our mandate to make disciples. On the other hand, the dialogue also scares me. My concern is that discipleship will become a fad like the fanny packs of the 1990s. (Aren't you glad those are gone?) To avoid this, we need to take steps to ensure that discipleship does not become another 40-day study or the program *du jour*. Understanding how information is integrated will hopefully temper our focus.

We all obtain skills through a process often referred to as the "Conscious Competence Ladder," or, as it is sometimes labeled, the "Learning Matrix." In addition to examining your pedagogical process, the matrix can assist you in coaching and discipling others in the learning process.

	Incompetence	Competence
Unconscious	Unconscious Incompetence	FLUENCY Unconscious Competence
Conscious	Conscious Incompetence	Conscious Competence LITERACY

Four stages comprise the rungs on the "Conscious Competence" sequence:

- Unconscious Incompetence,
- Conscious Incompetence,
- Conscious Competence, and
- Unconscious Competence.

Level 1 — Unconscious Incompetence
(You don't know that you don't know)

This is the stage often described by the aphorism "Ignorance is bliss." There are practices, principles, and skills that would empower you, but you have no clue they exist. You are unaware of the skills you need to succeed, and, sadly, you don't realize you lack them. This is often caused by a lethargic approach to biblical study or sheer pride. Don't let arrogance blind you to your weaknesses, and don't let laziness stand in the way of becoming biblically competent.

Level 2 — Conscious Incompetence
(You know that you don't know)

At this stage you realize your inabilities. Humility is the forerunner to this level of understanding. The longer you are in ministry, the more you discover skills you are lacking or areas in which you need to mature. Additionally, time with other believers helps you identify growth objectives in which to develop.

Level 3 — Conscious Competence
(You know that you know)

At this level you acquire knowledge, learn a skill, and implement what you know, fully aware of your abilities. This level is where you sharpen your skills and hone your craft through practice and discipline.

You create a powerful self-assessment tool by combining levels 2 and 3; you understand what you know and what you don't know. You are still concentrating on the performance of these activities, but as you get more practice and experience, these become increasingly automatic.

Level 4 — Unconscious Competence
(You don't know that you know)

At this stage your skills are performed with automatic ease. Skills in this level have been stored as habits, and they are executed subconsciously. In my experience, many believers operate in level 1 when it comes to disciple-making. Some pastors have been ringing the discipleship bell for years, but few people have listened.

Our ministry has hosted five discipleship conferences called *Replicate*, named after our ministry, with nominal attendance. The highest attended conference was in 2013, with just over 400. Those aren't impressive numbers in comparison to several larger conferences that attract over 8,000. Only recently has the discussion in larger venues turned toward discipleship. Now conferences such as *Exponential, Verge,* and *Multiply* are focusing on the topic of discipleship.

So why has it taken us so long to get here? There are at least three answers to this question: We don't know *that* we should engage in discipleship, we don't know *how* to engage in discipleship, and we don't know *why* to engage in discipleship. The easiest way for this mentality to change in the modern Christian landscape is for an army of disciples to rise up, filled with the Spirit of God and ready to take the command to make disciples seriously. Perhaps it can start with you!

Do you remember the staggering impact of exponential growth that we discussed in chapter 8? It's a slow process, but that's how God designed it. Discipleship is not a system based on "huge numbers, fast!" Rather, it is entirely dependent on human connection and an honest journey together. Once we are willing to grow together into the image of Christ, massive change will come.

CHAPTER 11

Why You Can't Disciple an Unbeliever

ONE OF THE MOST CONTROVERSIAL issues in discipleship today concerns our approach to working with unbelievers. After posting the statement, "You can't disciple an unbeliever," I was surprised by the mixed bag of responses I received from various people. Theologians, missiologists, and day-to-day practitioners are divided on this issue. And while it may seem as if we're splitting hairs in discussing it, I believe that understanding the nature of the person you're working with is as important as the *how* and *what* of your discipleship.

To understand why this question matters, we must travel back to the first century again. If you recall, the essence of discipleship back then was a commitment to study under a rabbi. Discipleship was focused on learning from the rabbi and walking in his steps. It was not just the memorization of facts or the learning of information. It included changes in lifestyle, giving up old habits and learning new ways to live and interact with others.

The goal of all discipleship is conformity to the image of Christ.

So how can you disciple someone, teaching them to be like their rabbi, without first introducing them to him? To be clear, I'm not opposed to *evangelism.* I encourage every follower of Jesus to meet with people who don't know Jesus — over coffee, lunch, or dinner. Find time to share your story with them, to introduce them to your rabbi. We should continue to share the gospel with unbelieving friends and teach the Bible to them. But let's not confuse evangelism with discipleship.

Let's define what we mean when we say "unbeliever." An unbeliever is someone who does not believe the gospel. The gospel calls us to repent of our sin and seek forgiveness on the basis of the death and resurrection of Jesus. We repent of our sin when we see it for what it is — an act of rebellion against our Creator and Lord. We believe the gospel when we hear the good news that Jesus has taken our punishment by paying the penalty our sins deserve and we love him — we decide that Jesus is more lovely and wonderful than our sin. So we reject our sinful patterns and worship God, grateful for what he has done for us.

An unbeliever has not trusted in the gospel, and as Ephesians 2 is clear, they cannot be discipled. As an unbeliever,

> You were dead in the trespasses and sins in which you once walked, following the course of this world, following the prince of the power of the air, the spirit that is now at work in the sons of disobedience — among whom we all once lived in the passions of our flesh, carrying out the desires of the body and the mind, and were by nature children of wrath, like the rest of mankind (Eph. 2:1–3 ESV).

Paul makes it clear: an unbeliever is spiritually dead in sin.

He elaborates on this further in his second letter to the church at Corinth when he writes,

> And even if our gospel is veiled, it is veiled to those who are perishing. In their case the god of this world has blinded the minds of the unbelievers, to keep them from seeing the light of the gospel of the glory of Christ, who is the image of God (2 Cor. 4:3–4 ESV).

Paul tells us that an unbeliever is blind to the gospel — they cannot see the "glory" or goodness of Christ. Instead, as Paul writes earlier in the letter, the unbeliever cannot "accept the things of the Spirit of God, for they are foolishness to him; and he cannot understand them, because they are spiritually appraised" (1 Cor. 2:14 NASB). Unbelievers are blinded to the beauty of Christ because they cannot yet understand the things of God. They have no ability to taste or discern what is true, noble, lovely, and beautiful, having a desire only for the pleasures of sin.

So, biblically it is clear that there is a divide between a believer and an unbeliever. But here is where it gets tricky. Which of us can judge the state of another man's heart? How do we determine if a person is truly born again, trusting in Christ for their salvation? The Bible gives us some guidance here as well, but it requires humility and discernment to judge wisely. Scripture tells us that the spiritual birthmarks of a person are the works they do. This does not mean that we are saved *by* our works. Rather, our works are the display of our salvation. We don't work *for* salvation; we work *from* salvation.

Diffusing the Confusion over Discipleship and Evangelism

Here is an image that may help you navigate the difference between evangelism and discipleship. Evangelism and discipleship are two oars attached to the same boat. With only one oar in the water, you will row in a circle. Both oars are required to navigate in a straight line to reach your destination. We need evangelism and we need discipleship to carry out the Great Commission. The gospel is received through evangelism and then lived out through ongoing discipleship.

So why is it so important for us to keep these two distinct? First, because the Bible maintains this distinction. Second, because when we make evangelism a part of discipleship, I believe we lose something. Our churches must retain an evangelistic emphasis, even as we cultivate and grow our discipleship efforts. Derwin Gray, pastor of Transformation Church in South Carolina, says it this way: "If our churches are not evangelistic, then our discipleship process has not been holistic."[1] We cannot make disciples the way Jesus intended if we do not engage in evangelism.

At this point, some might object and point us to the example of the twelve disciples of Jesus. It is difficult to pinpoint exactly when each of the first disciples believed in Jesus as the Messiah, the point when their true discipleship began. One of the problems in comparing ourselves to the original twelve is that they were looking ahead to the cross; we follow Jesus looking back to the cross. In addition, we must take into account the continued revelation of the Holy Spirit after the ascension of Christ. The first disciples received the Holy Spirit right after the Resurrection (see John 20) and then later on the Day of Pentecost, empowering them for mission and ministry. We today receive the Spirit the moment we place our trust and our lives in the hands of Jesus the Messiah.

What we share in common with the first disciples is the commitment to follow the same rabbi. In Mark 1:15, Jesus preached this message: "The time is fulfilled, and the kingdom of God is at hand [here]; repent and believe in the gospel" (ESV). In response, four fishermen — Peter, Andrew, James, and John — dropped everything, responded to the message, and followed Jesus immediately. The first disciples may not have fully understood the mission of Jesus, nor were they empowered by the Holy Spirit. But from the beginning they exercised faith in Jesus as the Messiah. They heard and believed that in this man was the coming of God's kingdom, and believing that good news, they followed him.

But that was not all. Following Jesus also involved repenting of their sin. We see this in the calling of Peter in Luke 5:7–11. Peter underwent a miraculous transformation in which he shifted from calling Jesus "Rabbi" to calling him "Lord." What changed for Peter? He recognized his sinful disobedience:

> They signaled to their partners in the other boat to come and help them; they came and filled both boats so full that they began to sink.
>
> When Simon Peter saw this, he fell at Jesus' knees and said, "Go away from me, because I'm a sinful man, Lord!" For he and all those with him were amazed at the catch of fish they took, and so were James and John, Zebedee's sons, who were Simon's partners.
>
> "Don't be afraid," Jesus told Simon. "From now on you will be catching people!" Then they brought the boats to land, left everything, and followed Him.

Peter met Jesus, saw the miracle Jesus performed, and was convicted of his sin. He knew that Jesus was no ordinary man.

The other disciples also recognized that Jesus was the Messiah. We read Andrew's, Philip's, and Nathanael's testimony upon meeting Jesus:

> One of the two who heard John speak and followed Jesus was Andrew, Simon Peter's brother. He first found his own brother Simon and said to him, "We have found the Messiah" (which means Christ)....
>
> Philip found Nathanael and said to him, "We have found him of whom Moses in the Law and also the prophets wrote, Jesus of Nazareth, the son of Joseph."...
>
> Nathanael answered him [Jesus], Rabbi, you are the Son of God! You are the King of Israel!" (John 1:40–41, 45, 49 ESV).

Perhaps a better example, one that more closely relates to our situation as Gentile (non-Jewish) believers after Pentecost, would be Paul's interaction with Festus and Agrippa, as told in Acts 25–26. Here we see Paul evangelizing by sharing his testimony and the message of the gospel. Paul is not discipling these unbelievers. He is preaching the gospel in the hope that the eyes of their heart will be enlightened to the truth. There Paul was not discipling these two unbelievers; he was evangelizing by sharing his testimony and the gospel. Discipleship involves an object and an objective. The object is Jesus. The objective is to be "conformed into the image" of Christ (see Rom. 8:29).

Let me bring it closer to home. If you had a neighbor who was a Hindu, you wouldn't say, "I'm discipling my Hindu neighbor who has an altar in his home devoted to his eight personal gods." You would say, "I am witnessing or sharing the gospel with my neighbor, with the hopes of him becoming a believer."

The reason we must keep this clear is that it affects how we interact with a person, what we expect of them. Until the Holy Spirit regenerates a person, he or she is hardened to the things of God, unable to take even one sanctifying step toward God. Remember how Paul describes our lives prior to regeneration:

- You were dead in your sins,
- You were actively practicing disobedience,
- You were seduced by the world,
- You were enslaved by Satan, and
- You were the object of God's wrath.

Being transformed into the image of Christ cannot involve any of these things, so the first step in discipleship must be to break unbelievers free from their unbelief — raising them to life through the gospel.

Go Therefore and Make Disciples

The Great Commission is not a logical order of steps. It's a set of three participles — go, baptize, and teach — all of which support the verb "make" with the same object "disciples." *Go* is not a one-time command. It describes a daily routine of life. You could say it this way: "As you are already going through life." Jesus anticipated our making disciples through the natural routine of life with the people around us.

And who are these people? They are believers. We should spread the gospel as we go, telling people about the hope that we harbor because of what God has done in Jesus Christ. After they respond, they will naturally have a hunger to be like Jesus. Discipleship is the step that comes next.

The Great Commission goes on to say that we should be "baptizing them in the name of the Father, Son, and the Holy Spirit." Jesus is not commanding us to make disciples and *then* baptize them. He assumes that we are discipling born-again, baptized believers.

Think about it. You don't baptize *unbelievers*. Baptism is like a "marriage certificate" that outwardly signifies the vows and commitments between a man and a woman. It's an outward expression of your inward desires, evidence that you intend to follow Christ. Baptism is an act of obedience that proceeds *from* salvation, not something that precedes it.

Trust and Obey

The primary item of business in discipleship is the final participle: "Teaching them to observe everything I have commanded you" (Matt. 28:20). Embedded in this phrase are a few truths worth noting:

- Discipleship must be centered on the Scriptures — the Bible is the textbook.
- Discipleship must involve teaching/preaching.
- Discipleship is more than transfer of information.

Jesus doesn't just say, "Teach them all my commands." He says, "Teach them to observe or obey all that I have commanded." Obedience isn't just a matter of knowing; it is a matter of doing. Today we would say that you need discipleship with accountability. Or we would talk about "holistic" discipleship that involves life transformation, where we spur one another on to observe and obey — to actually do what Jesus taught us to do.

Do you recall what Paul said to Timothy in 2 Timothy 2:2? Did he say, "What you have heard from me in the presence of many witnesses entrust to *unbelievers*"? No way! It reads: "What you have heard from me in the presence of many witnesses, entrust to *faithful men* who will be able to teach others also." You could rephrase Paul's words here to say, "Entrust to born-again believers the truths of the Christian life that you heard from me."

In Whom Are You Investing?

I want to close with a question. Since unbelievers are dead in their sin, seduced by the world and enslaved by Satan, what would you disciple them in? Would you teach them to be moral? To be a good person? Would you encourage them to be fair, to be a better citizen, a better father or mother?

There is a place for all of this. God has given common grace for the establishment of laws that order society, and even unbelievers can have a sense of the moral law, of the expectations of God written upon our heart. But these qualities, albeit worthy qualities to possess, are not what constitute Christian discipleship. Without a changed heart, a sinner remains separated from God and destined for a Christless eternity. Before people can be discipled, they must be saved and transformed by the Holy Spirit. We must evangelize the lost and disciple the saved.

Again, this requires a dose of humility and a measure of grace. Ultimately, only God knows who is saved and who is lost. But we must, at times, make judgment calls based on a person's lifestyle and their patterns and habits. We can look at what they love and value and how they are developing into men or women of character over time. Jesus instructed us to do this, to examine the fruit of someone's life to determine the root of their heart (Matt. 7:17). On more than one occasion, men in my D-Group, after weeks of studying, memorizing, and journaling through God's Word, have said to me, "I don't think I'm saved. I realized now for the first time in my life that I am lost. I need Jesus!" That's the power of God's Word at work!

Don Wilton, a pastor and a friend of mine, once shared with me a story from his early years on the seminary campus of New Orleans Baptist Theological Seminary. He had moved with his wife, Karin, to New Orleans from South Africa to train for ministry, and one of his first jobs on campus was as a painter. Wilton recalls discussing the gospel with a fellow seminary student as they stripped the walls and layered them with fresh paint. As they talked, the student fell under the conviction of the Holy Spirit and confessed to Wilton that he wasn't a believer. This was a man who had moved to the school to prepare for ministry. He was serving in a position of leadership at a church. But that day he realized that he didn't know Jesus.

Wilton led the burdened student through a prayer of repentance and confession. With tears in his eyes, the young man hesitantly asked Wilton a simple question: "What do I do now?" Wilton wisely responded, "You walk to the registrar's office, resign from Seminary, and move back home."[2] This man had just met Jesus for the first time, and he clearly was incapable of representing him in full-time vocational ministry. He needed to be discipled within a local church before he could take on the responsibility of discipling others.

Sadly, this is more common that we might think. Ministers can fall into the trap of loving the *ministry* of Jesus while neglecting the *Jesus* of the ministry. Wilton saw that this man was embarking on a discipleship journey with Jesus, not refining one he had already been on.

Raising the Standard

I know that all of this will sound harsh to some reading this book. Didn't Jesus allow anyone who approached him to join his disciple-making movement? Well, the simple answer to that question is "no, he did not." Read the Gospels again and notice that he selected twelve, but he also rejected thousands. Jesus refused to lower the requirements for following him. Quite the contrary, when the multitudes praised him, he raised expectations and drove them away.

Jesus expected his disciples to follow his example. And he understood that this would mean a high level of commitment to the Father and to his mission. Luke records Jesus' interaction with three men on the roadside, men who had misguided expectations about Jesus and what it meant to follow him.

The first potential follower assumed Jesus was a superstar rabbi who enjoyed the luxuries of the best hotels. But Jesus sharply corrected his self-serving view, replying, "Foxes have dens, and birds of the sky have nests, but the Son of Man has no place to lay his head" (Luke 9:58).

A second would-be disciple was willing to follow Jesus only after his father died. Recognizing this man's desire to receive his inheritance rather than forsake all for the kingdom of God, Jesus sternly answered, "Let the dead bury their own dead, but you go and spread the news of the kingdom of God" (Luke 9:60).

A third man approached Jesus. On the surface, his request appeared sincere. He said, "I will follow you, Lord; but first let me go back and say goodbye to my family." Seeing through the man's empathetic words to the real motive of his heart, Jesus tersely replied, "No one who puts a hand to the plow and looks back is fit for service in the kingdom of God" (Luke 9:61–62 NIV). This man had a misdirected focus.

Two glaring truths leap out at us from the pages of Scripture. First, Jesus must be first in your life. He will never settle for second place. He demands unwavering commitment. You must love him supremely, above everyone and everything else. Leonard Ravenhill, the revivalist from years past, said, "Anything you love more than Jesus is an idol."[3]

Second, Jesus never reduced the requirements for would-be disciples. He elevated them (see John 6). The story of the rich young ruler (Matt. 19:16–22) is a perfect illustration of this. Jesus responded to the man's initial question about eternal life as any good rabbi would — with a question: "Why do you ask Me about what is good?" He then proceeded to quiz the man about his conduct, asking him how well he had kept the commandments of God.

"'I have kept all these,' the young man told Him. 'What do I still lack?'"

Jesus leaves the man with a heart-piercing proposition: "'If you want to be perfect,… go, sell your belongings and give to the poor, and you will have treasure in heaven. Then come, follow Me.' When the young man heard that command, he went away grieving, because he had many possessions."

Jesus was not interested in the man's money; he was interested in his motivation. So he watches the man walk away — what may be one of the saddest verses in the Bible. This man was physically close to Jesus, and he may have even led an outwardly moral life, yet his heart was committed elsewhere. Unlike most pastors today, Jesus didn't call out to the man with a compromise to keep him engaged: "Okay, just sell half of what you have and then come follow me, and we'll see where you go from there." Nor did he weaken his challenge: "Come back … I've changed my mind.

Just get rid of a third of your possessions and follow me." And of course, he did *not* say, "Sell everything and give it to *me*." No. Jesus kept the bar high. Jesus didn't want the man's resources. He wanted his heart.

Jesus wants the same from us as well. Divided allegiance is a serious problem. It's grounds for ineligibility in the kingdom of God. Believers cannot say *no* and *Lord* in the same sentence.

Your Time Is Valuable

All of this raises a practical question. How selective should you be when choosing who to disciple? You may ask, "Should I enlist the first person who approaches me about participating in a D-Group, or should I be selective?" Well, yes and no. Before embarking on a yearlong journey with someone, pray about it. Pray for the person, and ask the Lord for wisdom and guidance. Jesus spent an entire night in prayer before formally calling the twelve to follow him (Luke 6:12–13).

Go slow in choosing potential group members. Your time is valuable, and as a steward of God's resources (including your time), you must use it wisely. This illustration has helped me with this in the past. Let's say that I offer you $86,400 today to spend on whatever you desire with one stipulation: you have to spend all the money today. What's left over will be forever lost. You cannot carry over today's money to tomorrow. Could you do it? Most of you are nodding your heads right now. "Of course, I could spend it." Amazon packages would be primed and ready for shipping. You may select purses, PS4 games, iPads, watches, cars, and clothes. You might even give a few bucks to charity. The list would be endless in your quest to spend every last penny you possess.

After your spending frenzy, let's say I show up the next day with the same offer: "Here is another check for $86,400 dollars to spend on whatever you want. But the same stipulations apply. Whatever you fail to spend will be wasted forever." Could you do it two days in a row? Of course, you could. Stock investments, debt retirement, and savings accounts would be filled with money.

God gives each one of us 86,400 seconds each day. We are free to spend them in whatever manner we wish. And when they're gone, they're gone.

Since time with your D-Group is limited, making the most of it is crucial. You must be judicious in selecting group participants, and grace must permeate the process. Remember how Jesus responded to the would-be disciples and the rich, young ruler. Look for those who are hungry and eager to learn. Seek out evidence that God is working in their heart and in their life. Disciple those who know Jesus and want to know what it means to follow him.

The great cricket player turned missionary, C. T. Studd, said it well: "Only one life, 'twill soon be past. Only what's done for Christ will last."[4]

Spend your life wisely. You only get one.

CHAPTER 12

Can I Make Disciples?

ISAAC NEWTON'S FIRST LAW OF motion states that an object at rest tends to stay at rest unless a force acts upon it. Unfortunately, this law is an accurate explanation for the state of the church today. Too much of the church is asleep, resting comfortably. And unless something acts upon it, the church will likely remain that way. In conversations with other pastors, I have heard several of them lament about the lackadaisical attitude of their church members. "No one is interested in growing deeper in their faith!" "I can't get my people involved in a small group." Many of these same pastors struggle to identify leaders in their church. But all of these problems are connected. The lack of leadership isn't a leadership problem, it's a discipleship problem.

Sometimes I'll probe a little deeper. "When do you meet with *your* discipleship group," I ask them. Their response is revealing: "Uh … *my* discipleship group? I don't have one; I'm too busy pastoring the church!" Congratulations! We have identified one of the primary problems. *You can't expect what you don't emulate.* Leadership requires that you lead by your own example.

Dealing with Our Doubts

One of the most confusing sentences in the Bible is Matthew 28:17, which says, "When they saw Him, they worshiped, but some doubted." At face value, it appears some of the most committed of Jesus' disciples doubted him. They had followed him for years, had witnessed his death, and had seen him raised to life.

And now they were doubting in the presence of the resurrected Jesus. What were they doubting?

Keep in mind that Jesus has already appeared to many of them on three other occasions (John 20:19–23; 20:24–29; 21:1–23). Some of them would even have remembered him predicting this very moment. They broke bread with him. They listened to his teaching. So how could they still doubt?

Typically, the word *doubt* means that we question the reliability of something or someone. The BDAG Lexicon, however, suggests that there may be an alternative way of understanding this verse. It tells us that doubt can also mean that one is "uncertain about taking a particular course of action."[1] Basically, it means "to hesitate." So put yourself in the disciples' shoes for a moment. You have been hunkered down in a room with the doors barred shut. Your leader has been brutally beaten and murdered. You aren't sure what has happened, even as you see him standing before you again.

While some of the disciples may have doubted the *identity* of Jesus, I am convinced that the majority of them doubted *themselves*. They hesitated. They second-guessed their ability and their own strength. Worship begins with a reverent fear of God; doubt begins with a fear of man. These disciples were asking themselves, "Can we really do this?" They wondered, "Do we know enough?" "What if they don't listen?" "What if they imprison us?" Or worse, "What if they kill us?"

How does Jesus respond to their doubts about the Great Commission? He comforts them with these words: "All authority has been given to Me in heaven and on earth" (Matt. 28:18). His words directly address their doubts. He affirms his authority and lets them know that he is sharing that authority with them. They have what it takes to carry on in the footsteps of their Master.

Jesus diverts their attention from their own inability to his sovereignty. In three verses (18–20), he uses the inclusive word *all* four times: (1) Jesus possesses *all* authority, (2) he commissions us to *all* nations, (3) we are to teach people to obey *all* he has commanded, and (4) he will be with us *all* the days (or always). The providence and presence of God bookend the Great Commission: "All authority has been given to Me" … "I am with you always, to the end of the age."

We may have doubts. But Jesus has authority and gives that to us. Simply put, he says, "Do what I ask, and I will be with you."

Large and In Charge

Our children learned a phrase during Vacation Bible School a few years ago about the authority of God: *"He's large and in charge."* Sometimes the simplest phrases have the greatest impact on us. Jesus' authority extended from heaven to earth. Mark's gospel communicates this message through several different situations in the life of Jesus.

First, we learn that Jesus had authority over the animal kingdom. Mark 1:13 says, "He was in the wilderness 40 days, being tempted by Satan. He was with the wild animals."

We all know that wild animals are dangerous to be around. But Jesus, as the text implies, wasn't afraid. As the creator of all things and the second Adam, Jesus has authority over the world He has made.

Jesus also has authority to teach, and those who heard Him recognized his authority. Mark 1:22 says, "They were astonished at his teaching, for he taught them as one who had authority, and not as the scribes" (ESV).

Imagine that you're in a literature class. Your professor is highly esteemed at the university and has been dealing with literature for more years than you've been alive. He expounds on the symbolic meanings of different characters, and you trust his reading because he's been studying it for a very long time. Now imagine that the author of the book walks through the door and starts talking about the very same things. You would immediately sense that the authority of the author is much weightier — because he wrote the book! The author isn't speaking about something that he's studied; he's speaking about something that he labored to create. That's what the crowds sensed when Jesus spoke. His authority was entirely different from the teachers' and scribes'.

Mark also tells us that Jesus had authority over the Sabbath. Mark 2:27–28 says, "He said to them, 'The Sabbath was made for man, not man for the Sabbath. So the Son of Man is lord even of the Sabbath'" (ESV). The misconception of the day was that the Sabbath was special in itself. The Sabbath was a sign of the special relationship the Jewish people enjoyed with God, a sign of the covenant God had made with them on Mount Sinai through Moses. But Jesus tells us that he is the one who created the Sabbath, and he made it for man.

Jesus reminds us that he is the one to whom the entire Old Testament points, and in his coming he has come to serve us — not to increase our load. Jesus reverses the common teaching of the scribes and teachers of the law and tells the people that the Sabbath is for us. We were built with the need to rest after our labors. We need to recharge after long weeks. God knew this when he created us, so he had us set aside a time to get that rest. The Sabbath was not made for God. It's not something he needs. It was made for man, who does need it!

Finally, Jesus tells us that he has authority to give authority. Mark 3:14–15 says, "He also appointed 12 — he also named them apostles — to be with him, to send them out to preach, and to have authority to drive out demons."

Jesus extended his authority to those who would come after him. He possesses the authority to give authority. Time and time again, Jesus demonstrated his authority to his disciples. This reminds us that God's sovereignty is the foundation for our own motivation to make disciples. If we do not believe God has a plan and is able to bring that plan to completion, that he is in control of all circumstances, we will be paralyzed with fear — fear of failure, fear of setbacks, fear of disappointment, and fear of inadequacy. Instead of fearing a future of failures, believers should possess a healthy fear of God. Jesus told his disciples,

"Do not fear those who kill the body but cannot kill the soul. Rather fear him who can destroy both soul and body in hell. Are not two sparrows sold for a penny? And not one of them will fall to the ground apart from your Father. But even the hairs of your head are all numbered. Fear not, therefore; you are of more value than many sparrows" (Matt. 10:28–31 ESV).

If Jesus has the whole world in his hands, as the children's song teaches, do you not think that you can trust him with the work of your hands? Billy Graham famously said, "The will of God will not take us where the grace of God cannot sustain us."[2]

If our service on the mission field is a reflection of our insistence to fear God, not man, then we are likely to encounter situations that would ordinarily terrify us to the point of paralysis. But because of the magnitude of the calling to which we're called, and because of the authority of the one who called us to it, we find that the freedom and life we crave may just be in a place we'd *never* go on our own.

We Serve in Christ's Authority

I have heard believers say to me, "I'll never go to Africa," or "I'll never go to the homeless shelter," or "I'll never go to the inner city." And then they go. And often they discover their life's purpose. For the first time, they realize what they were created to do.

If we believe that Christ has all authority in heaven and on earth, we should be open to anything and anywhere God is leading. We should be quick to say "Here I am, Lord; send me!" in response to his voice. Are you willing to go to China, Ukraine, Egypt, or Iraq with the gospel message? Are you willing to go to the nations? Are you willing to go to your neighbors?

The life you have always wanted may be in the mission you have always dreaded.

When Jesus enlisted the disciples to participate in ministry, he bypassed the elite teachers of Israel and the trained theologians in favor of average, ordinary people. He offered the disciples a promise that would sustain them through each of their various trials: "And remember, I am with you always, to the end of the age" (Matt. 28:20).

According to tradition, every disciple except John would be martyred for their faith in Christ. James the son of Zebedee, the older brother of John, was the first to die by beheading at the hands of Herod Agrippa. Matthias, who filled the vacant place of Judas as one of the twelve, was stoned before being beheaded in Jerusalem. Tradition holds that Andrew, Peter's brother, was crucified on an X-shaped cross because when he was going to be executed, he felt unworthy to be killed in the same manner that Jesus was. Angry pagans beat Bartholomew before enduring crucifixion.

Thomas the honest seeker traveled to India with the gospel. After a season of ministry, pagan priests tortured him and ran a spear through his body before tossing him into an oven of flames. Matthew traveled to Ethiopia. Instead of receiving his message with open arms, they pinned him to the ground and beheaded him.

Peter, the apostle Jesus restored on the Sea of Galilee, was stretched out on a cross to face a similar death as his master. Before the cross was placed in the ground, Peter demanded that the cross be turned end for end so he would be crucified upside down and not die in the same way as Jesus. Paul, the Apostle to the Gentiles, laid his neck on an execution block and was beheaded by Roman soldiers.

The greatest apologetic for the message we share is the list of men who knew Jesus better than anyone else and then voluntarily endured death for his sake. How were they able to tolerate persecution and suffer death? Jesus' words were on their hearts and minds constantly. They knew that regardless of what the earthly authorities did to them, there was only one who was really in charge. And he was the one they served. All authority belongs to Jesus Christ. In life and in death, we acknowledge that his purposes will be accomplished, that nothing is impossible or difficult for him. When Jesus said, "I am with you always, to the end of the age," every one of them understood that he would be with them in every circumstance, struggle, and joy.

The Future Is in the Past

One Saturday morning, a husband was watching a football game on television while waiting for his wife to get ready. They were preparing to visit some of their family. The team he was pulling for needed two touchdowns to win, and there were less than two minutes left on the clock. Miraculously, the team came from behind and scored twice, with the final touchdown in the last seconds of the game. The man's wife came down soon after that, ready to leave, unaware that her husband had been watching the game.

As they drove down the road, the wife was skimming through the radio stations and stumbled upon a rebroadcast of the game. Her husband turned to her, with two minutes left in the game, and said, "I bet you that we come back and win this."

"You're crazy," his wife replied. "There are only two minutes left, and we need two touchdowns!" She stressed over every tick of the clock, clinging to every one of the announcer's words as her husband drove down the road without a hint of anxiety. "Why aren't you getting nervous," she asked. "This is a really close game!" He assured her that he had faith that his team would win.

As the team threw the last-second pass to win, the wife, now exhausted from the anxiety of the thrilling finish, looked at her husband and asked, "Why weren't you worried?" He let her in on the secret: "I knew the outcome already."

The point of this story is that it might look at times like we are losing ground. The church may seem on the verge of capitulation. But we know that is not the future. We have a promise made to us by the one who rules all things. He will never leave us or forsake us, and he's coming back one day to forever establish his kingdom and claim what is his. We have nothing to fear because we know how the story ends. Jesus wins. And because we know this, we do not need to fear. We can do what Jesus asks us to do, confident in the outcome.

Yes, there will be days of discouragement. Your group may argue and disband. Someone you disciple may backslide or leave the church. But don't be discouraged. Remember that the one who defeated death sits on God's throne, and he is the one who calls you to make disciples. In his grace and through his power, we will do what he has asked us to do. We are never closer to Jesus than when we are doing what he commanded us to do. His final words, "Make disciples," should be our first work.

CHAPTER 13

MARCS of a D-Group

MY GOAL IN THIS BOOK has been simple, to rediscover an understanding of discipleship that has largely been lost in our churches today. We have covered a significant amount of ground together. We have rediscovered the differences between the Hebrew and Western mindsets, we have examined the history of discipleship and have seen how faithful men and women gave their lives to disciple others, and we have discussed the necessity of having a long-term commitment to disciple-making in a culture that demands immediate results.

Now, as we conclude, it is time to get into some of the practical details. As I mentioned earlier, every church needs to fit and adapt the principles of Jesus to fit the culture of the community. What works in Chattanooga may not work in Los Angeles, and vice versa. At the same time, it is helpful to have a place to start, to learn from what others have done and see how the process they have established might inform our own. In this closing chapter I want to offer a process that you can take with you as you begin making disciples.

In 1940, George Reavis wrote a short, twenty-four-page fable called *The Animal School*, in which a collection of animals band together to begin a school. They offer classes in running, tree climbing, swimming, and flying, and the reader is taken on a humorous and satirical journey through their educational process. The rabbit performs well in running, for instance, but is sent to remedial swim classes for how far it is behind the fish in swimming.[1]

The tale is written like a children's story as a call for educational reform, but it highlights a key idea: the metrics you use to determine success or failure should match the nature of the process and the purpose for which it was designed. You cannot judge a rabbit's aptitude at *rabbitness* by how it performs against a fish in a swimming race. Since disciple-making is an exponential process, judging the success of a discipleship model after two years by comparing it to the ministry of a busy evangelist is like comparing apples and oranges. In the context of our discussion here, we might say that the success of a D-Group should not be judged by a metric that was not designed for it.

So what are the appropriate metrics we should use to determine the success or failure of a D-Group? To engage in discipleship the way the Master intended it, I believe a D-Group should include these five principal elements. It should be:

- Missional
- Accountable
- Reproducible
- Communal
- Scriptural

It's convenient that these come together to form a handy acronym. I refer to these five characteristics as the MARCS of a D-Group, and not one of these "marks" is more important than another. The MARCS will provide an excellent starting point for you as you prayerfully consider beginning your own D-Group. Let's unpack each of them a bit further.

MARC #1: Missional

On the Sunday after Passover, the disciples were huddled together behind closed doors fearful of the world outside. Their leader had been murdered, and the religious leaders of the day were hunting his followers down. Suddenly, in their midst, Jesus appears. "Shalom," he says to them. "Peace to you."

Having said this, He showed them His hands and His side. So the disciples rejoiced when they saw the Lord.

Jesus said to them again, "Peace to you! As the Father has sent Me, I also send you" (John 20:20–21).

For the second time, Jesus comforts his disciples with that word: *shalom*. And then he gives them their marching orders. Many people speak of the Great Commission in Matthew 28:18–20, yet they neglect the First Commission Jesus gives here in John 20:21: "As the Father has sent Me, I also send you." Jesus reminds his disciples that their mission is to be modeled after his own. It's a rescue mission. He expects them to follow in his footsteps, to treat people as he has treated them, to do the things that he has been doing.

What comes next is very interesting. Jesus enlists his followers in a mission, and then he empowers them for ministry by breathing on them. "After saying this, He breathed on them and said, 'Receive the Holy Spirit'" (John 20:22). The disciples are drafted and then equipped.

Did you catch the connection between the words *breathed* and *Spirit*? These two words are synonymous in the Hebrew language. *Ruah* can be translated as spirit, wind, or breath, depending on the context. The first occurrence of the word is found in Genesis 1:

In the beginning God created the heavens and the earth.

Now the earth was formless and empty, darkness covered the surface of the watery depths, and the Spirit of God was hovering over the surface of the waters (Gen. 1:1–2).

In his encounter with Nicodemus at night, Jesus describes the regenerating work of God in salvation by likening the Holy Spirit to the wind that created the heavens and the earth.

"The wind blows where it pleases, and you hear its sound, but you don't know where it comes from or where it is going. So it is with everyone born of the Spirit" (John 3:8).

But the first thing the disciples would have thought of as Jesus breathed on them was the scene in Genesis where God creates Adam and breathes his life into him:

> The LORD God formed the man out of the dust from the ground and breathed the breath of life into his nostrils, and the man became a living being (Gen. 2:7).

God breathes his life into his disciples and gives birth to his church. It is a reminder to us that we cannot accomplish the mission of Jesus without the one who empowers the ministry — the Holy Spirit.

Over the years, I have been amazed at some of the misunderstandings I have encountered about the work of the Holy Spirit. After I preached on the Holy Spirit in Colorado Springs, one man waited in line to talk with me and started out saying, "I know you Baptists don't believe in a filling of the Holy Spirit like we do."

I immediately stopped him there: "You must have misunderstood what I just spoke about. Of course I believe in a filling of the Holy Spirit. I even believe in a *second* filling of the Holy Ghost."

With a surprised look on his face, he inquired, "You do?"

"Of course I do!" I said. "And a third filling, and a fourth filling, and a fifth."

Paul discouraged believers from being intoxicated with wine. Instead, he exhorted the church at Ephesus to be "filled with the Spirit" (Eph. 5:18 ESV). As I explained to this man, Paul envisions us being continually filled with the Holy Spirit, day after day. It's not just an event that happens once or twice; it's an ongoing practice, a part of growing and maturing into a disciple of Jesus.

So what is the purpose of these fillings of the Spirit? Rather than something that draws attention to us or that is primarily about speaking in indiscernible languages, it's a means of empowering us for the ministry of Jesus. The Greek word *pimplemi* — usually translated as "filled" — means to be full or satisfied. In context, then, a person who is "filled" is someone "wholly imbued, affected, influenced with or by something."[2]

The gospel of Luke and the book of Acts are written by the same author, essentially one book divided into two sections. Both of these are letters addressed to someone called Theophilus (Luke 1:3; Acts 1:1), and they are loaded with references to individuals "filled with the Spirit" or "full of the Holy Spirit." By my count, there are eight instances where this phrase is used.

We are spending all of our time in this section on Missional living discussing the Holy Spirit because what happens *after* the Spirit fills believers in the New Testament is always the same — they boldly proclaim the Word of God. Don't believe me? Take a look at the twelve occurrences of the filling of the Holy Spirit in Luke-Acts.[3]

1. Luke 1:13–15 — John the Baptist was prophesied to be filled with the Holy Spirit for the purpose of preparing the way for the Messiah.

2. Luke 1:39–41 — Elizabeth was filled with the Holy Spirit to proclaim with a loud cry to Mary, "You are the most blessed of women, and your child will be blessed!"

3. Luke 1:67 — Zechariah was filled with the Holy Spirit to prophesy and set the stage for the ministry of his son, John the Baptist.

4. Acts 2:2–4 — The disciples were filled with the Holy Spirit to speak in intelligible tongues so that the diverse group of people in town for the Passover feast could understand them.

5. Acts 4:7–8 — Peter was filled with the Holy Spirit to preach a sermon which saw 3,000 converts.

6. Acts 4:31 — A crowd of believers was filled with the holy Spirit after hearing Peter and John's report of being released from persecution by the Sadducees.

7. Acts 9:17 — Ananias laid hands on Paul, who was then filled with the Holy Spirit to speak boldly about Jesus in the synagogues.

8. Acts 13:8–11 — Paul was filled with the Holy Spirit to speak boldly to the sorcerer Elymas and in turn astound the proconsul with truth and persuasiveness.

In every occurrence, the filling of the Holy Spirit is followed by an *immediate* proclamation of God's glory, either through prophecy, speaking in foreign tongues, or hugely receptive Spirit-filled preaching. The filling of the Spirit is not a reason for people to marvel at us; it is entirely for God's glory and proclamation. Jesus promised that the Spirit would glorify him (John 16:14), and the very same Spirit will empower us to speak boldly on his behalf.

Every believer has been entrusted with the task of being "witnesses in Jerusalem [our community], in all Judea [our surrounding region] and Samaria [our surrounding country], and to the ends of the earth [the world]" (Acts 1:8). A healthy D-Group keeps the mission front and center. We are called to live as witnesses for God, reflecting his image to a lost world around us. To do this, we must be filled with the Holy Spirit. The Spirit empowers us to proclaim the truth about Jesus in our words and in our actions. A witness is a walking billboard, projecting a message that advertises the good news about Jesus to the world around us.

Missional living happens when D-Group participants are held accountable to build *intentional friendships* and engage in *lifestyle evangelism*. Encourage your group members to be intentional in their neighborhoods — often the most overlooked mission field we have — at their workplaces, around their lost friends, and in the presence of their family members.

What does this mean, practically? It means that you shouldn't rush to get inside after getting home from work. Linger outside to see if God has set up any divine appointments with your neighbors. Look for opportunities for God to open the door to share the gospel. Befriend others, but don't attach strings to the relationships. Take an interest in others.

The gospel frees us from being preoccupied with ourselves. Exercise your freedom by asking others questions about their life. Listen more and talk less. Dale Carnegie, in his book *How to Win*

Friends and Influence People, understood this principle when he said, "You can make more friends in two months by becoming interested in other people than you can in two years by trying to get other people interested in you."[4]

Don't Miss Divine Appointments

Slow down long enough to recognize where God is working around you. I was recently convicted about the way I was handling my Bible reading time each night with my boys. My two sons, Rig and Ryder, love this time together. With extra sips of water, late night snacks, toy cleanup, and teeth brushing, some nights take longer than others before they finally get to bed. Often, in my haste, I scurry the boys off to bed.

One night, as I was kneeling in the dark next to Rig's bed, he said to me, "Dad, we forgot to do our quiet time."

"Son, we are doing quiet time," I responded. "It's called sleep."

But that wasn't the answer he wanted to hear. "Daddy, we forgot to read our Bible story." My son wants to read the Bible. What am I going to say? So I turn on the lights and pull out the Bible to read.

Still, I'm in a hurry to get it done. I'm glossing over entire paragraphs when the kids aren't watching, and I'm skipping pages to shave off a few minutes. Rig, who knows the Bible accounts by heart, lets me know: "Daddy, we missed a page." What should be a priority for me — a focused time of reading the Bible with my children — had become a task for my nightly checklist. Another thing to get done. As you can imagine, I was convicted.

Sadly, our approach to evangelism can become like this as well. You can't rush the Holy Spirit. You can't control where God is going to work and how long he is going to take. And we have to remind ourselves of what is important. Opportunities for sharing your faith are everywhere if you look for them. Challenge your D-Group participants to slow down and live intentionally. Encourage them to rely on the Holy Spirit for strength. Missional living needs accountability.

Resist the temptation to view those around you as projects or boxes to check on your spiritual checklist, which tends to become a means of trying to earn favor before God, a subtle form of works-righteousness. Instead, live out the freedom of the gospel and genuinely display the love of Christ. People aren't projects. But that doesn't mean you can't pray for them. Ask them about their struggles and intercede for them. Pray for their hearts to be receptive to the gospel. Ask God for an open door to share your testimony with them.

Mack Stiles, in his small book *Evangelism*, suggests meeting with lost friends to read the Bible together.[5] If "faith comes from hearing, and hearing through the word of Christ" (Rom. 10:17 ESV), reading the Word will soften the hearts of hardened sinners to accepting the gospel. As we mentioned earlier, this isn't a regular D-Group, since the nature of the gathering is evangelistic. By sharing the word and praying for the person, your hope is that they will eventually submit to Christ as both savior and Lord.

Every form of evangelism begins with prayer. We must call upon the one who opens blinded eyes and clogged ears to hear and see that the Lord is good. Two spiritual parents, as with human conception, must be present for spiritual birth to take place: the Holy Spirit and the Word of God. Through prayer and Scripture reading, God may open the hearts and minds of lost people for repentance and faith. Because God is the author of salvation, success in our evangelistic efforts is in the sharing, not the saving.

Here are six specific ways to pray for your lost friends and family:

1. That they seek to know God. God has good plans for their lives — "plans for welfare and not for calamity to give you a future and a hope" (Jer. 29:11 NASB). He promises to reveal himself and his plans to those who seek him wholeheartedly (see Acts 17:27; Deut. 4:29).

2. That they believe the Scriptures. A non-Christian does not naturally understand the gospel. You must pray that the

Holy Spirit will give them the understanding to believe the truth of God's Word (see 1 Cor. 1:18).

3. That God will draw them to himself. We must always remember that although God uses us as the instruments to share the message and help lead people to him, only he can convict and convert them. One cannot receive Christ until God first draws him. Let us therefore pray that God will draw our friends to him (see John 6:44).

4. That the Holy Spirit will work in them to turn from their sin and follow Christ as Lord. Be willing to let God work in their lives (Luke 15:17–18). Be bold enough to pray that God will cause things to come into their lives that will cause them to seek him (see Prov. 20:30; John 16:8, 13; Acts 3:19).

5. That God will send someone to lead them to Christ. Perhaps that someone is you. Pray that God will give you boldness to speak to them about Christ. Before you pray this prayer, be sure you mean it and will obey the Lord (see Rom. 10:14–15; Matt. 9:37–38).

6. That they believe in and confess Christ as Savior and Lord. It is important that people understand that, in receiving Christ as Savior, they are also making him the Lord of their lives. Pray that they will understand the seriousness of the commitment to receive Christ. Pray that they will come to grasp the scope of God's love. As their loving Father, He will never ask them to give up anything without giving them something far better in return. (see John 1:12; Rom. 10:9–10).

MARC #2: Accountable

When I was saved on November 12, 2002, God redeemed me from a $180-a-day heroin and cocaine addiction.[6] My counselor encouraged me to attend an Alcoholics Anonymous meeting every day for the next ninety days. Yes, ninety days in a row! But there was a good reason for that. The successive daily pattern of attending the meeting eliminates distractions in your life as you build up days of sobriety, all of which will hopefully ensure success.

When a person commits to a program like Alcoholics Anonymous, one of the first things they're encouraged to do is find a sponsor. The role of a sponsor is to provide an example of sobriety and encourage the person in their recovery. Essentially, this person holds you to your commitment in attending the meetings, as well as asking the tough questions about personal, day-to-day struggles.

Alcoholics Anonymous has a clear process for recovery, and it has stood the test of time. I recently uncovered one of the final interviews conducted with AA co-founder Bob Smith in 1948. In this interview, Smith made some impressive statements about the Bible:

> In the early days ... our stories didn't amount to anything to speak of. When we started in on Bill D. [Bill Dotson was the third participant of the program], we had no Twelve Steps either; we had no traditions. But we were convinced that the answer to our problems was in the Good Book.... It wasn't until 1938 that the teachings and efforts and studies that had been going on were crystallized in the form of the Twelve Steps. I didn't write the Twelve Steps. I had nothing to do with the writing of them.... We already had the basic ideas, though not in terse and tangible form. We got them, as I said, as a result of our study of the Good Book."[7]

Now I should say at the outset that the contemporary Alcoholics Anonymous is not what it used to be. Over the years, political coercion from activists groups and government intervention has led AA to remove the name of God from their literature and to substitute it with words like "higher power." At Brainerd Baptist Church, we offer a Christ-centered recovery program similar in many respects to AA called Celebrate Recovery.

Yet, despite the deviations from the roots that started the movement, two identifiable markers are still present, and they are the key to AA's longevity. First, the entire plan is built on an accountability group. You are expected to show up for the weekly, bi-weekly, or daily meetings. You are held accountable by friends so that you are never alone on the journey. Second, every person who works in the program is assigned a qualified sponsor. Each group provides coaching and support through a life-on-life model. The sponsor is there to direct, equip, support, and delegate.

Does any of this sound familiar? It should. It's quite similar to the model of rabbinic discipleship we see in the New Testament. In the original discipleship group, Jesus was the sponsor, and the twelve disciples were participants in his accountability group. After sending his disciples out on two occasions to do the work by themselves, Jesus inquired about their missionary endeavors. Each reported on all they had seen and done (see Luke 9 and 10).

I believe the AA accountability system works because each member is held to a standard, one that is clearly set before them. In a D-Group, it's no different. Every D-Group begins with clear standards and expectations. In our groups, the participants sign a covenant as an affirmation of their commitment. Here is the one I use:

———

I will commit to the following expectations:

- *I pledge myself fully to the Lord with the anticipation that I am entering a time of accelerated spiritual transformation.*
- *I will meet with my D-Group for approximately one-and-one-half hours every week, unless providentially hindered.*
- *I will complete all assignments on a weekly basis before my D-Group meeting, in order to contribute to the discussion.*
- *I will contribute to an atmosphere of confidentiality, honesty, and transparency for the edification of others in the group as well as my own spiritual growth.*
- *I will pray every week for the other men/women who are on the discipleship journey with me.*
- *I will begin praying about replicating the discipleship process upon completion of this group.*

———

The lesson we learn from AA is that you can expect much from the men and women you disciple, and you can use accountability to ensure that they meet those expectations. Hold them accountable to the standard you set by ensuring that week-to-week accountability is in place.

Here are eight accountability questions you can ask your D-Group members:

1. Have you spent time in the Word and in prayer this week?

2. Have you shared the gospel or your testimony with an unbeliever this week?

3. Have you spent quality time with your family this week?

4. Have you viewed anything immoral this week?

5. Have you had any lustful thoughts or tempting attitudes this week?

6. Have you told any self-promoting lies or half-truths this week?

7. Have you participated in anything unethical this week?

8. Have you lied about any of your answers today?

If you cultivate a culture of honesty, trust, and transparency in your group, you will experience the power of discipleship in ways you never thought possible. Remember, what gets measured gets accomplished. *Don't expect what you don't inspect.*

MARC #3: Reproducible

All around the world you will hear workers serving up chicken orders with the words, "It's my pleasure." Chick-fil-A is one of the most successful businesses in the United States, and there are a few things they can teach us about training disciples. For instance, every employee of Chick-fil-A endures a rigorous month-long training regime. This training serves a dual purpose: educating and retaining. The entire process they use is reproducible, down to the final words you hear at the window after receiving your six-piece "Christian nuggets." *Every* employee, *everywhere* repeats the phrase "my pleasure." Listen for it the next time you receive your drink.

I raise this because it highlights the third MARC we need to measure: reproduction. If you claim to be a follower of Christ, but you are not working to help others become followers of Christ also, are you taking Jesus' words seriously? A disciple follows Christ. Jesus didn't say, "Come follow my religion," "… my denomination," or "… my preacher." He invited people to walk in his footsteps, imitate his actions, and carry out his commands.

Paul understood that the life of a disciple-maker should be reproducible. To the Philippian church he wrote, "Brothers, join in imitating me, and keep your eyes on those who walk according to the example you have in us" (Phil. 3:17 ESV). The word *imitate* simply means to copy. Paul didn't expect the Philippian Christians to become exact clones, doing everything he did. He asked them to *follow him in his pursuit of Jesus.* He wanted them to emulate his general conduct and his way of life, a life characterized by walking in Jesus' footprints.

Paul's ultimate goal was not for them to follow him, but to follow Christ. He explains this in his first letter to the church at Corinth, writing, "Follow my example, as I follow the example of Christ" (1 Cor. 11:1 NIV). Discipleship wasn't a theoretical discussion for the eleven men who followed Jesus. They gave their lives for the gospel, following in the footsteps of Jesus.

The truth is that you may never fully realize the impact of your ministry because it may come through another person. We see this in the relationship between Moses and Joshua. Moses invested his time and energy into Joshua. And even though God gave Moses the vision, the mission, and the plan, Moses himself never set foot in the land promised by God. He never experienced that final victory. He dealt with the persistent complaints from the people, their nagging about starvation from lack of food and thirst from no water. Joshua, on the other hand, was the one who entered the land and annihilated the enemy. He tasted and experienced all that the Lord had promised. Moses started something, but God finished it without him.

Also consider the example of Elijah. Elijah called down fire from heaven, experienced miraculous multiplication of food with a widow and her son, and prayed for rain to stop and start again. But God also let him know that he would give a double portion to the man who would come after him — the one Elijah would invest in. The Bible records that Elisha performed twice as many miracles as Elijah did.

Jesus invested his life into twelve men. He led a full-time, itinerant ministry for three years. Yet, at the end of His life, Jesus said, "Truly, truly, I say to you, whoever believes in me will also do the works that I do; and *greater* works than these will he do, because I am going to the Father" (John 14:12 ESV, emphasis mine). These "greater works" are not more significant — who could do anything greater than God? — but rather have a broad scope and reach. Jesus' ministry was intentionally restricted to Israel for three years. The twelve disciples would take the message to the ends of the earth.

One Person Can Make a Difference

A pastor was overjoyed at his role in the conversion of one man, and he shared it with a denominational director. The director didn't think much of it, since only one conversion had happened in the church. He asked, "Why are you so excited about this one man coming to the Lord, pastor? Shouldn't you have better numbers than that?"

The pastor didn't listen to the director. He continued to pour his life into this man, teaching him the Bible, how to study and memorize it for himself. They prayed together, ministered together, and lived together.

After several years of being invested in, this man went on to make an impact for the kingdom of God. His name was F. B. Meyer, the evangelist and Baptist pastor. Charles Spurgeon, the

"Prince of Preachers," once said of him, "Meyer preaches as a man who has seen God face to face." Meyer preached more than 16,000 sermons in his sixty-year ministry.

What would have happened if the pastor hadn't invested in him? How different would countless believers' lives be? The truth is, we just don't know. We will never know if we are discipling the next F. B. Meyer, Charles Spurgeon, or Billy Graham. So we don't focus on the numbers; we focus on the mission: reproducing. Live a life that is worth imitating, and then give it away by sharing it with others. You grow best when you give away what you have.

The discipleship process is not complete until the mentee becomes a mentor to others. The player should become a coach. Here are a few steps you can take to increase the likelihood that your group will be MARCed by reproduction:

- Sign a covenant at the outset of the group, which includes a line about replicating at the end of the process. (See the Appendix for an example.) Don't spring this expectation onto participants at the end of the process.
- Remind members to take notes throughout the process. You never learn for yourself. You are learning for the person who will come after you.
- As members near the completion of the group, have them list names of potential future D-Groups participants for prayer before they approach them.
- Encourage members to approach the potential participants.

MARC #4: Communal

Community is often used synonymously with the word "fellowship" or the Greek *koinonia*. It is a quality that develops when men and women unite around a common interest — in this case, around the gospel. Someone once defined fellowship as "two fellows in the same ship." We share a common destination, a common purpose in our union with others. And it is natural for us to desire community, because this is the way we were designed.

Mike Breen, in his book *Building a Discipling Culture*, tells the story of Danny Wallace and his attempt to create community.[8]

Wallace, a television producer in London, learned one day that his aged great-uncle, Gallus Breitenmoser, passed away in Switzerland. At the funeral Wallace made a discovery that would change the course of his life. Gallus's family members were laughing about a crazy idea that he had but never saw fulfilled.

Just after World War II, Gallus had become disillusioned by gossip, slander, and general disgust of his city and dreamed of escaping from it. Fortunately, he owned some land, so he decided to start a community farm. He got out the word and hoped there would be one hundred other people who wanted to join him on this farm. Imagine his disappointment when he only got three.

Upon hearing this tale, Wallace decided to revive the farm and make it a reality, out of loving memory for his uncle. He put an ad in a local paper and soon received his first applicant: a waiter in a restaurant in his part of London. Wallace put up a website and soon exceeded Gallus's goal of one hundred people to join him. The interesting aspect is that he never told them what it was they were joining; they were simply wishing to be included in whatever it was that he had going on.

Wallace soon realized that he was going to have to give purpose to the group. He sent out an email with instructions: they were to take one day of the week, Friday, and use it to do good in their community. Give sandwiches to the homeless, help sort food at a shelter, leave a big tip for a waiter who is having a rough day. He called these days Good Fridays, and their collective the Karma Army.

A D-Group meets a fundamental human need. We want a place to belong. Participants should have a sense of unity because we are living life together — not for karma, but for Christ. Remind those in the group that we are not working for the here and now; we exist for eternity. Professor D. A. Carson makes clear the uniting power of the gospel when he says,

[The church] is made up of natural enemies. What binds us together is not common education, common race, common income levels, common politics, common nationality, common accents, common jobs, or anything else of that sort. Christians come together ... because they have all been saved by Jesus Christ. They are a band of natural enemies who love one another for Jesus' sake.[9]

The story of Jesus links us together into a chosen nation with one God and a common history. We are children of Abraham, united by a promise about a people who would one day number the grains of sand on the earth and the stars in the sky. God's promise was a vision for a *community* — his people.

In Jesus' day, salvation would not have been primarily thought of as a singular and individualistic experience. Salvation was, first and foremost, corporate and plural. The kingdom of God is not a collection of isolated individuals. It is a gathering of individuals united together in Christ. And all of us are united by a common purpose, playing a role in the spread of God's kingdom and its exaltation of Jesus Christ.

Today there are people who claim to be believers, yet they celebrate their detachment from the church. They claim to read the Word, pray, and worship, but they don't have any affiliation with a local gathering of believers. They say, "I'm not into worship gatherings. I don't practice organized religion. I just can't do that church thing." But this is like saying, "Robby, I love you. We're tight. You're my closest friend in the world. But I hate your family and don't really want to associate with any of them."

That doesn't fly with me. Jesus gave his life for the church, not for just a random collection of individuals. The church is his vision for our salvation — we are saved from ourselves *into* his family, his bride. The church may look like Shrek (an ogre), but it's still the bride of Christ.[10]

The Bible is replete with passages urging disciples to live out their faith in community. In the New Testament we find clear commands urging us to follow Jesus in community with other believers. Here are just a few of the many "one another" Scriptures we find:

- Love one another. (John 13:34)
- Be in agreement with one another. (Rom.12:16)
- Accept one another. (Rom. 15:7)
- Instruct one another. (Rom. 15:14)
- Greet one another. (Rom. 16:16)
- Serve one another. (Gal. 5:13)
- Be kind and compassionate to one another. (Eph. 4:32)
- Submit to one another out of reverence for Christ. (Eph. 5:21 NIV)
- Admonish one another with all wisdom. (Col. 3:16 NIV)
- Encourage one another and build each other up. (1 Thess. 5:11)
- Confess your sins to one another and pray for one another. (James 5:16)
- Be hospitable to one another. (1 Pet. 4:9)

While some of this can be practiced on a Sunday morning, in reality, a D-Group is an ideal setting for living out many of these commands. For example, consider confessing your sins. Larger contexts such as Sunday school or small groups aren't well suited for this. But it's something we need to do regularly, since sin festers and grows in isolation. A D-Group is significantly less threatening for addressing sins, and believers may be more apt to open up about present struggles in this context.

Dietrich Bonhoeffer emphasizes the dangers of isolation: "Sin demands to have a man by himself. It withdraws him from the community. The more isolated a person is, the more destructive the power of sin over him."[11] This is why participation in a group is essential. The concept of a "passive participant" doesn't make sense either. Everyone comes prepared to contribute. Through community with like-minded brothers and sisters in a discipleship setting modeled by the Master, spiritual growth is made possible, but only insofar as it is based on the firm foundation of God's Word.

MARC #5: Scriptural

Spangler and Tverberg, in *Sitting at the Feet of Rabbi Jesus*, write of the importance of Bible study:

> Would it surprise you to learn that the rabbis thought that study, and not prayer, was the highest form of worship? They pointed out that when we pray, we speak to God, but that when we study the Scriptures, God speaks to us.[12]

The basis for all things — worship, community, action, and faith — is the Word of God.

Consider for a moment just how crucial the Word of God is. The apostle John says, "In the beginning was the Word, and the Word was with God, and the Word was God" (John 1:1). The Word is inseparable from God, because the Word is God himself. God the Father speaks, and the Word that he speaks creates. The Word rushed from God's mouth and established the heavens and the earth, separated light from dark, and sprang everything that there is into existence.

"How can a young man keep his way pure?" asks the Psalmist in Psalm 119. "By keeping Your word" (v. 9). In order to follow in the steps of the Savior, we must obey the things that he has said.

A prophet's job in the Old Testament was to recite the Words of God to the people with perfect clarity and lucidity. Isaiah begins his book with these words: "Listen, heavens, and pay attention, earth, for the LORD has spoken" (1:2). In Isaiah 55:11, God promises, "My word that comes from My mouth will not return to Me empty, but it will accomplish what I please and will prosper in what I send it to do." Likewise, Jeremiah, after the introductory comments, begins, "The word of the LORD came to me" (1:4). Sixty times in the book of Ezekiel we find the phrase, "The word of the LORD came to me." The same phrase is used by the prophets Hosea, Joel, Amos, Micah, Zephaniah, Haggai, and Zechariah. In your hands, you hold thousands of pages of the very voice of God speaking to you.

Sadly, some discipleship ministries use everything but the Word in their weekly gatherings. One group in Chattanooga questioned what they saw as our overemphasis on the Bible in our discipleship. They asked us: "Why don't you read men's books? Men need practical, real world truths to apply their lives." Our answer was simple: "The Word of God contains all the practical, real world advice a man needs. When you get in the Word, you learn how to be a better father, a better parent, and a better follower of Christ."

At Brainerd, we say, *"Get into the Word until the Word gets into you."* The Bible is the textbook. That's why the last mark in the MARCS of a D-Group is being Scripture-based. We emphasize three things by this:

- *Study* the Scriptures slowly,
- *Journal* the Scriptures daily, and
- *Memorize* the Scriptures weekly.[13]

MARC Your Groups

A D-Group isn't a magical formula for success. That's why we need the MARCS — clear "marks" that define how we will measure success and failure in our discipleship. If you have a collection of like-minded individuals who are intent on being missional and accountable, reproducing themselves, worshipping God through community, and studying God's Word together, you have a recipe for success in discipleship. You have a context in which to prayerfully work your way through difficult passages in the Bible. You have brothers and sisters to hold you up in your quest to be like Jesus.

Discipleship is the goal. God has called us to make disciples, and this means evangelizing unbelievers, welcoming them into his kingdom, and then discipling them to grow closer to the perfect example set for us by his Son. This is not a fancy program to purchase or a rigid, Pharisaical system of rules to follow. Discipleship is a journey alongside like-minded brothers and sisters to be conformed to the image of Christ.

Best of all, we aren't alone. You are never closer to Christ than when you are doing what Jesus commanded us to do. Why not get started today!

Conclusion

THOMAS WAS A DISCIPLE OF Jesus. History tells us that at the end he gave his life for his rabbi and for the message of the gospel. Yet, today we remember him negatively for a scene after the resurrection where he doubts that Jesus has really been raised from the dead. Thomas's name has even become a bit of a slur, somewhat akin to a "Negative Nancy" or a "Gloomy Gus." To call someone a "Doubting Thomas" suggests that they are irrationally firm in their disbelief.

So what did Thomas say that has forever put him in such a negative light? He said, "If I don't see the mark of the nails in His hands, put my finger into the mark of the nails, and put my hand into His side, I will never believe!" (John 20:25). This is the unfortunate legacy that Thomas gets left with.

In light of this, I want to encourage you to take a fresh look at Thomas. Far from being a negative example for us, I believe Thomas is a shining example of what a disciple should look like.

The Scene

Let's go back to that moment after the resurrection again. It is the first day of the week, a Sunday. Some women return from Jesus' tomb with surprising news. They proclaim that the body of the Messiah is missing. Peter and John, unconvinced by the testimony of the women, run to see it for themselves and then return to their homes, leaving the weeping Mary by herself at the tomb. The next thing they know, Mary is searching the town to find them, ecstatic that she has had an encounter with the risen Lord.

That same night, the disciples are gathered together in a locked room. The news that Mary has shared is buzzing in the air, mixed with their apprehension of Jesus' words that they would be persecuted alongside him (John 15:20). It has been an unforgettable weekend.

Suddenly, there is another man in the room. Jesus is standing among them. He speaks peace to them, breathes on them, and fills them with his Spirit. Then he commissions them to go and continue the work he has begun on earth.

Notably absent from the gathering is Thomas.

We are not sure precisely where Thomas is, but it can be reasonably assumed that after the traumatic death of his Lord and the threat of political action against some of the disciples, he is lying low. Or he is overcome with emotion and just wants to be alone. Whatever the case, Thomas is not in attendance that night.

Now, imagine what he must have felt when his fellow disciples raced out to tell him what had happened. He may have thought they were crazy. Or they were trying to lift his spirits. He responds by letting them know that he won't be fooled again. He will need to put his hand in the marks where the nails and spear had been driven before he believes again.

Eight days later, the disciples convene again, likely in the same room where they met Jesus the previous week. They have locked the door, have settled into their fellowship, and are most likely telling Thomas, who is with them this time, about their experience again.

What do we know of Thomas? We know a few things.

First, we know that *he was devoted to live with Jesus*. We are first introduced to Thomas in John 11 as Jesus prepares to raise Lazarus from the dead in Bethany. Jesus receives the news of Lazarus while he is still in Jericho. When Jesus announces to His disciples that He is going to make the journey, they warn Him against going, reminding Him that the religious leaders tried to kill Him last time.

Jesus says that He is going anyway, despite the danger. Thomas unflinchingly speaks up: "Let's go so that we may die with Him" (John 11:16). Thomas's words here display his enormous devotion to Jesus. He is committed to Jesus completely.

Second, we know that *Thomas desired to learn.* John mentions Thomas one more time before Jesus' death. Thursday night in the Upper Room, after Jesus washes the disciples' feet, he speaks some perplexing words:

> "Your heart must not be troubled. Believe in God; believe also in Me. In My Father's house are many dwelling places; if not, I would have told you. I am going away to prepare a place for you. If I go away and prepare a place for you, I will come back and receive you to Myself, so that where I am you may be also. You know the way to where I am going" (John 14:1–4).

The disciples, sitting in silence, contemplate what Jesus has just said. Thomas, speaking for the group, says, "Lord, ... we don't know where You're going. How can we know the way?" Jesus tells him, "I am the way, the truth, and the life. No one comes to the Father except through Me" (John 14:5–6). Notice that Thomas has asked an honest question. Jesus never turns away a sincere person seeking truth. Everyone else sat dumbfounded while Thomas stepped forward. He genuinely wanted to know what Jesus was talking about. He had a desire to learn the Truth.

I know that I would rather have someone ask a simple question and risk looking foolish than for them to remain in the dark. This tells us that Thomas was an independent thinker. He was a thoughtful man who contemplated Truth, who wrestled with all the facts, and considered every implication before placing his trust in Jesus.

Third, we see that *Thomas' doubt led to his belief in Jesus.* As you can imagine, the days leading up to Thomas' famous expression of doubt were nothing short of a roller coaster. He had his feet washed by the Son of God, he prayed in the Garden of Gethsemane, he watched Peter slice an ear off of a Roman guard, he witnessed one of his brothers — Judas — sell out the group and their Leader. And he watched Jesus, shackled and mocked, get beaten mercilessly before hanging on a cross to die.

People grieve in two ways: publicly and privately. Some want to be around a company of friends and family to talk everything out and get it off their chests. Others want to be alone so that they can think and pray. Thomas preferred the latter. He had to get away to process everything and was not present when Jesus appeared to the others the first time.

Here is a man who gave Jesus everything he had, and he is now brokenhearted by Jesus' departure. Thomas's expression of doubt was not the profession of an unbelieving cynic; it was the grieved desperation of a distressed believer. He was willing to believe in the return of his Master, but he was unable to do it. He didn't have enough evidence to justify it in his head.

When Jesus met him, Thomas didn't need the physical evidence he had demanded a week earlier. Previously, he had said that he wouldn't believe until he put his hands in Jesus' wounds. Yet the second he sees the risen Savior, he exclaims, "My Lord and my God!" We have no record of him ever touching Jesus' wounds. Nevertheless, this makes him the first disciple to acknowledge Jesus' divinity after the resurrection.

Our Authority in Christ

Many of us are like Thomas. We want answers to our questions before we commit to something. And that is *just fine*. In fact, it can be good. Those who have asked questions are being honest about their doubts. They are bringing them into the light and allowing room for God to speak truth to them.

Thomas should motivate us all to take the baton and run with it. He had a front row seat on the hillside when Jesus issued His last words to His eleven followers. He heard his rabbi proclaim, "All authority has been given to Me in heaven and on earth" (Matt. 28:18). He overcame his doubts and placed his faith in the risen Savior.

Not only does Christ have all authority, but he also has authorized our message. He has given us the words to preach and pass on to others. No other religious leader or group can claim that. The Anglican pastor John Stott states,

The fundamental basis of all Christian missionary enterprise is the universal authority of Jesus Christ, "in heaven and on earth." If the authority of Jesus were circumscribed on earth, if he were but one of many religious teachers, one of many Jewish prophets, one of many divine incarnations, we would have no mandate to present him to the nations as the Lord and Savior of the world. If the authority of Jesus were limited in heaven, if he had not decisively overthrown the principalities and power, we might still proclaim him to the nations, but we would never be able "turn them from darkness to light, and from the power of Satan unto God" (Acts 26:18).[1]

Since Jesus conquered sin, death, hell, and the grave, we have no reason *not* to go to the nations with an unstoppable message.

So what are you waiting for?

You have a victorious Savior, a secured salvation, a mandate to make disciples, and a process for carrying it out.

"Therefore, go ..."

APPENDIX

Frequently Asked Questions about Discipleship

How Do I Choose Disciples?

The first step in establishing a formal disciple-making relationship is choosing disciples. Jesus, our example in selecting disciples, spent time in prayer before selecting men (Luke 6:12–16). Begin by asking God to send you a group of men or women who have a desire to learn and grow.

When people approached Jesus about becoming his disciples, our Lord held a high standard. One man said, "First let me go bury my father" (Luke 9:59). Understand that the man's father had not yet died; he wanted to wait until after his father died. Jesus said something like, "You can't do that. The kingdom is too important. We do this now, or we don't do it at all."

Like Jesus' relationship with his disciples, ours is a serious relationship, built upon a mutual commitment to Christ and each other. Tragically, some will not follow through with that commitment, forcing you to confront them about their unfaithfulness.

Occasionally it may become necessary for you to ask someone to leave the group. In my years of leading D-Groups, on two occasions I have had to let go of an unfaithful group member by saying, "Listen, I love you, brother. I want to work with you, but at this stage in your life, your actions are telling me this is not a good time. Maybe we can meet in the future, when you are at a different place in your spiritual walk."

As painful as this is, it sometimes happens. When it does, always be careful to handle it in a manner that edifies the uncommitted believer. Here are a few reasons for asking someone to leave the group: consistently missing the scheduled meeting times without a valid excuse; a combative personality that causes strife within the group; unrepentant, persistent sin, or moral failure, to name a few.

Your D-Group should consist of *F.A.T.* believers: Faithful, Available, and Teachable. A faithful person is dedicated, trustworthy, and committed. Consider a potential disciple's faithfulness by observing other areas of their spiritual life, such as church attendance, small group involvement, or service in the church. Faithfulness is determined by a commitment to spiritual things.

Discern an individual's availability by their willingness to meet with and invest in others. Does this person carve out time to listen, study, and learn from others? Is he accessible when called upon? Does she have a regular quiet time with God of reading the Word and praying? Availability is measured by a willingness to serve God.

Not everyone who attends a Bible study, Sunday school class, or D-Group is teachable. A teachable person has a desire to learn and apply what is taught. One who is teachable is open to correction. Recognize teachability by observing one's response to God's Word. For example, after hearing a sermon on prayer, does he begin to pray more regularly? Or after a lesson about the dangers of the tongue, does this person implement changes in her speech? A teachable person not only listens to what is taught, but also applies it to his or her life.

After discerning that an individual is faithful, available, and teachable, prayerfully approach him or her and ask, "Would you be interested in studying the Bible together? Would you be interested in memorizing Scripture and praying together?" I have personally found that many people are open to that. All you have to do is ask. Never say, "Would you like for me to disciple you?" as this question may come across in a derogatory manner. Also, keep in mind, men should disciple men, and women should disciple women.

When Should I Ask Someone to Leave the D-Group?

As I said, I have asked only two people to leave my D-Group in nine years. Someone should be asked to leave the group for reasons such as these: they don't possess a teachable spirit, or they are not faithful in attending or completing the assigned work.

Teachability is an indispensable quality for growth. In one situation, I asked a person to leave the group because he monopolized the discussion week after week. It was obvious he wanted to demonstrate his knowledge of the Word, rather than learn from interacting with others.

Additionally, laziness will breed complacency in the group. Missing meetings, refusing to memorize Scripture, failing to log journal entries, or sitting idly by during discussion times lowers the morale of the others in the group. This type of behavior must be addressed immediately. Meet with this individual privately to inquire about their attitude and actions. Remind them of the commitment made at the outset of the discipleship relationship.

Other reasons may require dismissing a group member. For example, a group member who is not trustworthy to maintain confidentiality or is judgmental toward others in the group may have to be removed.

How Many People Should Be in the Group?

Because accountability works well in a smaller setting, the ideal size of a disciple-making group is three to five — you and two to four other people. Never have more than six, and remember that a one-on-one relationship is not ideal. In the past I have tried meeting with a group of nine men. Building continuity in a group of that size was difficult. Opt for a smaller group if possible.

Where Should We Meet?

Find a meeting place away from the church. Restaurants, coffee shops, bookstores, diners, and homes are all good options. Meeting outside the church in the community forces your group to publicize your faith, teaching them that it is okay to read the Bible at a restaurant or to pray in public. Be sure to select a place that is convenient to all group members. I know stay-at-home moms who meet in each other's houses.

How Often Should We Meet?

Ideally, you should meet once a week. You can meet more frequently, but it is important that you meet at least once a week. This schedule does not prohibit those you are discipling from calling you throughout the week or coming by for counsel when needed. Discipleship is an all-the-time, 24/7 commitment. In addition to the weekly D-Group meeting, members are encouraged to enroll in a community/life group during the week for fellowship, community, and edification.

Should There Be an Attendance Requirement?

Yes, and it is not negotiable. The first time I meet with a potential group, I explain the disciple-making covenant with them. Since we're going to spend our lives together for the next twelve to eighteen months, I want to know if they are committed. Some people have said after the initial meeting, "Uh, this isn't really for me. I'm not interested." That's okay. I allow potential disciples to opt out of the group on the front end after understanding the expectations spelled out in the disciple-making covenant.

Remember, you are looking for people who *want* to be discipled, people who have a desire to grow and learn. An unwillingness to commit reveals that they are not ready to be a disciple or that immaturity on their part merits a different sort of discipleship. It's the example Jesus set for us.

What Should Our Meetings Look Like?

Begin with prayer. Ask each participant to present one prayer request at the start of each meeting. Assign a person to pray over the requests, and ask the Lord to sharpen each of you through your relationship.

Your weekly meetings should focus on four elements:

(1) Study the Word together. I have written an entire book on the H.E.A.R. method of studying the Bible: Highlight a passage, Explain it in context, Apply it to your life, and Respond in prayer. Following this method will drive the group discussion.

(2) Hold each person accountable for Scripture memory by reciting the previous week's passage before the group.

(3) Ask accountability questions of each other. Hold each person accountable for achieving their goals. For example, "How is your relationship with Linda? You mentioned last week that you were working on the way you spoke to your wife."

(4) Pray together before departing.

How Do I Dig Deeper into the Bible?

To study the Bible in depth, you will use some study tools, beginning with a Bible dictionary. Early in our disciple-making relationship, David Platt gave me a Bible dictionary for my birthday. He said, "Robby, here's a gift that you'll use." And he was right. In addition to a Bible dictionary, it is important to have a good study Bible. (The ESV Study Bible, the MacArthur Study Bible, and the NIV Study Bible include helpful commentary on each verse). If you can't afford to buy one of your own, you can access one on the Internet. Go to websites such as BibleGateway.com, Biblehub.com, Bible.org, or BibleStudyTools.org. These are great.

How Do I Challenge My D-Group to Memorize Scripture?

Proverbs 25:11 says, "A word fitly spoken is like apples of gold in a setting of silver" (ESV).

How many times has a Scripture come to mind when you needed just the right words in a situation? Jesus promised that the Holy Spirit would bring to remembrance all that Jesus said (John 14:26). Those passages of Scripture we have memorized will be brought to our memory at the right moment — but we must learn them. Group members will memorize Scripture if you hold them accountable through reciting verses to one another at every meeting.

What If I Don't Know the Answer to a Question?

I am often asked questions to which I don't know the answers. There is no shame in not knowing all the answers to every question. Simply confess that you may not have all the answers, but you will find them, and then do so before the next meeting. Ask your pastor or another spiritual leader to help you with the answer. Never give the impression that you have all the answers.

At the height of Henry Ford's popularity, people claimed that he was the smartest man in the world. During this time, a Chicago newspaper published a statement calling him an "ignorant pacifist." Ford fought the claim by suing the paper, which resulted in a trial, landing him on the stand. Attorneys asked Ford questions on every subject imaginable, none of which he could answer. Exhausted from the questions, Ford ended the examination by stating,

> If I should really want to answer the foolish question you have just asked, or any of the other questions you have been asking me, let me remind you that I have a row of electric push-buttons on my desk, and by pushing the right button, I can summon to my aid men who can answer any question I desire to ask concerning the business to which I am devoting most of my efforts. Now, will you kindly tell me why I should clutter up my mind with general knowledge, for the purpose of being able to answer questions, when I have men around me who can supply any knowledge I require?[1]

What he said was, "I am not the smartest man in the world because I know all the answers, but because *I know where to find the answers.*" You may not have total recall when it comes to biblical history, theology, and doctrine, but with time you can locate the answer.

When Do I Send Out Disciples to Make Disciples?

Always begin with the end in mind. Your group should meet for twelve to eighteen months. Some groups develop a closer bond, which results in accelerated growth; others take longer. The maximum time for meeting is two years. Some group members will desire to leave the group and begin their own groups. Others, however, will want to remain in the comfort zone of the existing group. Some will not want to start another group because of the sweet fellowship and bonds formed within the current group. Remember, the goal is for the men and women of the group to replicate their lives into someone else.

Paul, at the end of his life, commanded Timothy, "And what you have heard from me in the presence of many witnesses entrust to faithful men who will be able to teach others also" (2 Tim. 2:2 ESV). Within that one verse are four generations of disciple-making. Paul to Timothy is the first-to-second generation. Timothy to his disciples is the second-to-third generation. Timothy's disciples to others is the third-to-fourth generation. The goal of your group is to make disciples who will make disciples.

Jesus entrusted the greatest message in the world to twelve men, and one of them turned on him. As a result of the commitment and faithfulness of the remaining eleven men, you are reading this book today. Disciple-making was Plan A. Jesus handed the baton to the disciples when he said, "Go, therefore, and make disciples of all nations" (Matt. 28:19). The apostles handed it to the early church fathers, who handed it down through the centuries. And now, the baton has been handed to you.

Run with endurance! Eternity is at stake.[2]

Acknowledgments

I HAVE BEEN RESEARCHING, CATALOGING, and editing the material in this book for over a decade, so it goes without saying that there are many people to thank. I am indebted to the Replicate team — Tim Lafleur, Dave Wiley, Paul Laso, John Richardson, Kandi Gallaty, and Mollie Wiley — who meet every week to discuss practices, principles, and avenues for making disciples. I could not have written this book without your insights and encouragement.

I am grateful for those who contributed editorial comments: Hamilton Barber, Paul Laso, and Linda Brown. I am grateful for the men in my discipleship groups over the past few years: Casey, Jesse, Jason, Jody, Scott, Todd, Michael, David, Nathan, Corey, Bryan, Trey, Ryan, Billy, Jared, Jonathan, Wiley, Sean, Clay, Rupe, Dallas, Johnny, Jeff, Paul, Richard, Monte, Chad, Jim, Rick, Steve, Tom, Sherman, Miguel, Chris, Beau, Hamilton, Adam, Tom, Dean, Randy, and Doug. I learned more from you than I could have ever taught you.

I am very grateful for the members of Brainerd Baptist Church who spur me on to be a better pastor and disciple of Christ. You have taken the challenge to "Go make disciples" seriously.

I am grateful for the board members of Replicate Ministries. Many of you believed in me when no one else did. Your constant encouragement and support have encouraged me to complete this book.

I am thankful for my family: Kandi, Rig, and Ryder. You have sustained me in the writing, re-writing, and editing process. This book would not be a reality without your consistent support.

I am eternally thankful for the great salvation I have in Jesus Christ, for without Him none of this would be possible. His grace sustains me daily. I have never gotten over being saved on November 12, 2002.

Bible Versions

Endnotes

Introduction

1. Steve Murrell, *WikiChurch: Making Discipleship Engaging, Empowering, and Viral* (Lake Mary, FL: Charisma House, 2011), 27–28.
2. Check out Will Mancini's website Auxano.com for helpful discipleship resources, and his book *Intentional Disciplemaking*.
3. See Rick Warren, *The Purpose Driven Church: Growth Without Compromising Your Message & Mission* (Grand Rapids: Zondervan, 1995).
4. Liz Wiseman and Greg McKeown, *Multipliers: How the Best Leaders Make Everyone Smarter* (New York: Harper-Collins, 2010), Kindle Edition (Kindle Locations 331-335). (2010-06-03).
5. Ibid. (Kindle Locations 346-348).
6. Timothy Ferriss, *The 4-Hour Body: An Uncommon Guide to Rapid Fat-Loss, Incredible Sex, and Becoming Superhuman* (New York: Crown Publishing Group, 2010), Kindle Edition (Kindle Locations 482-484).

Chapter 1: The Master's Model for Making Disciples

1. William Manchester, *The Last Lion: Winston Spencer Churchill: Visions of Glory, 1874-1932* (New York: Bantam Books, 1984), 125.
2. Alexander C. Diener and Joshua Hagen, eds. *Borderlines and Borderlands: Political Oddities at the Edge of the Nation-State* (Lanham, MD: Rowman & Littlefield, 2010), 189. Churchill boasted in his later years that he created the Kingdom of Jordan "with the stroke of a pen, one Sunday afternoon in Cairo."

3. Shmuel Safrai, "Education and the Study of the Torah," in *The Jewish People in the First Century, Volume 2*, ed. David Flusser et al. (Boston: Brill Academic, 1988), 965.

4. Ibid., 945-70.

5. Marvin Wilson, *Our Father Abraham: Jewish Roots of the Christian Faith* (Grand Rapids: Eerdmans, 1990), 302.

6. Mishnah, Bava Metzia 2:11.

7. Norman H. Snaith, *The Distinctive Ideas of the Old Testament* (New York: Schocken Books, 1964), 184–85.

8. Avot 2:8

9. Steven Isaacs, "Hasidim of Brooklyn," *The Washington Post* (17 February 1974), B4.

10. Josephus, Against Apion 1.12 (60).

11. Wilson, *Our Father Abraham*, 299–300.

12. Roy Blizzard and David Bivin, "Study Shows Jesus as Rabbi" (25 February 2004), www.biblescholars.org.

13. See Robert Coleman, *The Master Plan of Evangelism* (Ada, MI: Revell, 2010); Bill Hull, *Jesus Christ, Disciplemaker* (Grand Rapids: Baker Books, 2004).

14. Ann Spangler and Lois Tverberg, *Sitting at the Feet of Rabbi Jesus: How the Jewishness of Jesus Can Transform Your Faith* (Grand Rapids: Zondervan, 2009), 51.

15. Ibid., 52.

16. Zig Ziglar, See You at the Top (1975; Gretna, LA: Pelican Press, 2005), 45.

Chapter 2: Think Like a Hebrew

1. See Richard Whitaker et al., *The Abridged Brown-Driver-Briggs Hebrew-English Lexicon of the Old Testament: From A Hebrew and English Lexicon of the Old Testament by Francis Brown, S.R. Driver and Charles Briggs, Based on the Lexicon of Wilhelm Gesenius* (Boston; New York: Houghton, Mifflin, 1906).

2. See Larry L. Walker, "Heart," in *Eerdmans Dictionary of the Bible,* ed. by David Noel Freedman, Allen C. Myers, and Astrid B. Beck (Grand Rapids: Eerdmans, 2000). Examples of the

words being used interchangeably can be found in the variations of translations (my emphasis in quotations below).

Compare Romans 1:21 (NLT): "Yes, they knew God, but they wouldn't worship him as God or even give him thanks. And they began to think up foolish ideas of what God was like. As a result, their *minds* became dark and confused," to Romans 1:21 (NASB): "For even though they knew God, they did not honor Him as God or give thanks, but they became futile in their speculations, and their foolish *heart* was darkened."

Another instance is seen in 2 Corinthians 9:7 (NRSV): "Each of you must give as you have made up your *mind*, not reluctantly or under compulsion, for God loves a cheerful giver," and 2 Corinthians 9:7 (NASB): "Each one must do just as he has purposed in his *heart*, not grudgingly or under compulsion, for God loves a cheerful giver."

3. Brian Knowles, "The Hebrew Mind vs The Western Mind," http://www.godward.org/hebrew%20roots/hebrew_mind_vs_the_western_mind.htm (accessed 20 July 2014).

4. Anytime you see "im" at the end of a Hebrew word, it signifies plurality.

5. Shmuel Safrai and Menahem Stern, eds., *The Jewish People in the First Century* (Amsterdam: Van Gorcum, 1976), 968.

6. Ray Vander Laan "A Far Country: Decapolis," http://www.followtherabbi.com/guide/detail/ a-far-country-decapolis: "Bargil Pixner, a noted scholar on Galilee, has pointed out an ancient religious tradition that helps clarify the Jewish view of the pagan Decapolis. He noted that in the Talmud and in the writings of the church fathers, the people of this area were described as belonging to the seven pagan Canaanite nations driven out of the Promised Land by Joshua and the Israelites (Josh. 3:10; Acts 13:19). These nations worshipped Baal and ate (and sacrificed) pigs (Isa. 65:3-5, 66:3). Apparently, the pagan practices of the people of the Decapolis and their anti-God values seemed to be continuations of the practices of the Canaanites, who used sexual perversions and even child sacrifice in their

worship. It is probable that the people of Jesus' day, who took their Scriptures seriously, viewed the Decapolis as very pagan. Although we do not know how many Jews actually believed that the people of the Decapolis were the descendants of the Canaanites, the fact that there is a link between the blasphemous practices of these two peoples helps establish the validity of this Jewish view."

7. After the people call Jesus "unholy" in Matthew 12:22–33, He speaks in parables from this point on, beginning in Matthew 13.

8. "Alexander the Great's March of Conquest," http://factsand-details.com/world/cat56/sub366/item2036.html (accessed 20 February 2015).

Chapter 3: A Picture Is Worth a Thousand Words

1. Dwight Pryor, *The Messiah and the Apostle* (Haverim study notes, 09 April 2007).

2. John J. Parsons, "Shavuot: Revelation and the Fruit of the Spirit" from Hebrew for Christians. http://www.hebrew4christians.com/Holidays/Spring_Holidays/Shavuot/shavuot.html

3. Dwight Pryor speaks of this concept in his book *Behold the Man: Discovering Our Hebrew Lord, the Historical Jesus of Nazareth* (Dayton, OH: Center for Judaic-Christian Studies, 2005).

4. Mishnah Pirkei Avot 1:4 states, "Yosi ben Yoezer of Tzeredah and Yosi ben Yochanan of Jerusalem received the Torah from them. Yosi ben Yoezer of Tzeredah said: Let your house be a meetinghouse for the sages and sit amid the dust of their feet and drink in their words with thirst."

Chapter 4: Disciple-Makers Are Made, Not Born

1. "Jesus Disciples a Teenage Posse." http://kbonikowsky.wordpress.com/2008/08/20/jesus-disciples-a-teenage-posse/ (accessed 20 July 2014).

2. Rick Duncan, founding pastor of Cuyahoga Valley Church in Ohio, emailed New Testament scholars from multiple denominations with a question. "What our youth pastor and I are asking

is this: 'If indeed it's true that the disciples were primarily teenagers (or that many of them were teenagers), then what are the implications for us as we pursue developing a discipleship culture in our churches today?'" The responses were divided somewhat evenly, with a slight edge in favor or a young adult stance.

3. Bill Hull mentioned this idea in a sermon he delivered at Brainerd Baptist Church on April 21, 2013, entitled, "Why Should We Bother with Discipleship?"

4. William Arndt, Frederick, W. Danker, and Walter Bauer, *A Greek-English Lexicon of the New Testament and Other Early Christian Literature* (Chicago: University of Chicago Press, 2000), 196.

5. See chapter 9 of my book *Growing Up: How to Be a Disciple Who Makes Disciples* (Bloomington, IN: CrossBooks, 2013).

6. Spiro Zodhiates, *The Complete Word Study Dictionary: New Testament* (Chattanooga, TN: AMG Publishers, 2000), Logos Electronic Version.

7. Joey Bonifacio, *The LEGO Principle: The Power of Connecting to God and One Another* (Lake Mary, FL: Charisma House, 2012), 16. Kindle Edition (2012-09-04).

Chapter 5: A Forgotten Practice

1. Molly T. Marshall, Review of *The LEGO Principle: The Power of Connecting to God and One Another* in *Review and Expositor* Journal, vol. 101 (2004), 70.

2. Bill Bright, *Revolution Now* (San Bernadino, CA: Campus Crusade for Christ, 1970), 195.

3. Ibid., 197. Bright is referring to the Universal Church.

4. Doug Hartman and Doug Sutherland, *A Guidebook to Discipleship* (Irvine, CA: Harvest House Publishers, 1976), foreword.

5. Augustine, *Confessions*, 6.15. http://www.ccel.org/ccel/augustine/confess (accessed 25 April 2014.)

6. Ibid., 8.5.

7. Ibid., 8.8.

8. Robert Clinton, *The Making of a Leader* (Colorado Springs: NavPress, 1988), 31, 89.

9. Edward Smither, *Augustine as Mentor* (Nashville: Broadman & Holman, 2008), 214.

10. Expositions in Psalms 99:9, English translation from Zumkeller, Augustine's ideal, 388.

11. Smither, *Augustine as Mentor*, 214.

12. Ibid., 216.

13. Augustine, *Letter*, 73.2

14. Augustine Sermon, 340.1. http://www.ccel.org/ccel/schaff/npnf106.vii.xxviii.html (accessed 25 April 2014).

15. For an expanded history of discipleship, check out Bill Hull, *The Complete Book of Discipleship: On Being and Making Followers of Christ*, in Navigators Reference Library (Colorado Springs: NavPress, 2006).

16. http://discipleshipgroups.blogspot.com/2006/02/models-of-discipleship-throughout.html

17. Alexandre Faivre, *The Emergence of the Laity in the Early Church* (New York: Paulist Press, 1990), 69.

18. Queen Mary was responsible for the murder of 300 Christians for their faith, the first of whom was John Rogers, who published his translation of the Bible in 1537 under the pseudonym Thomas Matthews.

19. Charles Spurgeon set aside a portion of the service for the pastoral prayer; so does Mark Dever, the contemporary pastor of Capitol Hill Baptist Church in Washington, DC.

20. Carter Lindberg, *The Pietist Theologians* (Malden, MA: Blackwell Publishing, 2005), 40.

21. J. I. Packer, *Honouring the People of God: Collected Shorter Writings of J.I. Packer on Christian Leaders and Theologians* (Vancouver, BC: Regent College Publishing, 2008), 250.

22. Charles Haddon Spurgeon, *C. H. Spurgeon Autobiography: The Early Years (1834–1859)*, rev. ed. (Edinburgh: The Banner of Truth Trust, 1976), 417.

23. Peter White, *The Effective Pastor: The Key Things a Minister Must Learn to Be* (Ross-shire, UK: Mentor, 1998).

24. Richard Baxter, *The Reformed Pastor* (1656; reprint, Edinburgh: Banner of Truth Trust, 2007), 177.

25. Ibid., 226.

26. Jonathan Edwards, "Farewell Sermon." http://www.ccel.org/e/edwards/works1.i.xxvi. For more on Richard Baxter, see Timmy Bristers Blog: http://timmybrister.com/2008/11/who-is-richard-baxter.

27. Daniel Walker Howe, *The Making of the American Self: Jonathan Edwards to Abraham Lincoln* (Cambridge: Harvard University Press), 1977, 38.

28. Sereno E. Dwight, *Memoirs of Jonathan Edwards*, in *The Works of Jonathan Edwards*, vol. 1 (1834; reprint, Edinburgh: Banner of Truth Trust, 1974), xxxvi.

29. George M. Marsden, *Jonathan Edwards: A Life* (New Haven, CT: Yale University Press, 2004), 133.

30. Matt Perman, *What's Best Next: How the Gospel Transforms the Way You Get Things Done* (Grand Rapids: Zondervan 2014), 162. http://whatsbestnext.com/2011/06/the-resolutions-of-jonathan-edwards-in-categories/

31. *The 70 Resolutions of Jonathan Edwards, 1722–23*, in S. E. Dwight, *The Life of President Edwards* (New York: G. and C. and H. Carvill, 1830), 68.

32. Iain D. Campbell, *Heroes and Heretics: Pivotal Moments in Twenty Centuries of the Church* (Fairn, Scotland: Christian Focus, 2004), 10.

Chapter 6: A Band-Aid for the Church

1. Dissertations dealing specifically with Wesley's preaching are scarce. However, there are numerous papers dealing with his doctrine, theology, and ecclesiology.

2. James Hall, "An Account of Mr. James Hall, Written by Himself," in *The Arminian Magazine* 16 (1793): 287.

3. Gladwell, Malcolm, *The Tipping Point: How Little Things Can Make a Big Difference* (Boston: Little, Brown, 2006), Kindle Edition (Kindle Locations 2060-2065).

4. I would differ with Wesley on his perspective of man's depravity, the responsibility of man, and sinless perfectionism, to name a few points of contention.

5. Kevin Watson, *The Class Meeting: Reclaiming a Forgotten (and Essential) Small Group Experience* (Wilmore, KY: Asbury Seedbed Publishing, 2013), Kindle Edition (Kindle Locations 368-370).

6. Paul Lee Tan, *Encyclopedia of 7700 Illustrations* (Garland, TX: Bible Communications, 1996), 110.

7. Henry D. Rack, *Reasonable Enthusiast: John Wesley and the Rise of Methodism* (Philadelphia: Trinity Press International, 1989), 532.

8. Stephen Tompkins, *John Wesley: A Biography* (Grand Rapids: Eerdmans, 2003), 44.

9. Al Bryant, *The John Wesley Reader* (Waco, TX: Word Books, 1983), 56. This entry was recorded on February 12, 1772, according to Wesley's memoirs.

10. Richard J. Payne, *John and Charles Wesley, Selected Writings and Hymns* (Ramsey, NJ: Paulist Press, 1981), 9.

11. Alister E. McGrath, ed., *The Blackwell Encyclopedia of Modern Christian Thought* (Malden, MA: Blackwell Publishers, 1993), 87.

12. Albert C. Outler, *John Wesley* (New York, NY: Oxford University Press, 1964), 11.

13. Tompkins, *John Wesley: A Biography*, 43.

14. Ibid., 44.

15. James Lawson, *Deeper Experiences of Famous Christians* (New Kensington, PA: Whitaker House, 1998), 87.

16. Basil Miller, *John Wesley* (Minneapolis: Dimension Books, 1983), 24.

17. Dennis H. McCallum, "Phillip Jacob Spener's Contribution to Protestant Ecclesiology," 1989. http://www.xenos.org/essays/

phillip-jacob-speners-contribution-protestant-ecclesiology (accessed 15 February 2014).

18. D. Michael Henderson, *A Model for Making Disciples* (Nappanee, IN: Evangel Publishing House, 2005), 61.

19. John Whitehead, *The Life of the Rev. John Wesley with the Life of the Rev. Charles Wesley* (Boston: Dow and Jackson, 1845), 292.

20. George Whitefield, *Journals* (August 1738; reprint, London: Banner of Truth Trust, 1960), II: 50.

21. Henderson, *A Model for Making Disciples*, 109. Wesley's meticulous journal entries affirm this.

22. Elton Trueblood, *The Best of Elton Trueblood: An Anthology* (Kirkwood, MO: Impact Books, 1979), 34.

23. Mark Galli and Ted Olson, eds., *131 Christians Everyone Should Know* (Nashville: Christianity Today, 2000), 183. Wesley's structural innovation did not end with the infrastructure. "In 1787, Wesley was required to register his lay preachers as non-Anglicans. To support the American movement, Wesley independently ordained two lay preachers and appointed Thomas Coke as superintendent. With these and other actions, Methodism gradually moved out of the Church of England — though Wesley himself remained an Anglican until his death."

24. John Wesley, *The Works of John Wesley*. vol. 8 (Nashville: Abingdon, 1989), 300.

25. Henderson, *A Model for Making Disciples*, 108.

26. Ibid., 112.

27. David Hempton, *Methodism: Empire of the Spirit* (New Haven, CT: Yale University Press, 2005), 79.

28. John Wesley, *The Works of John Wesley*, vol. 2 (Nashville: Abingdon, 1988), 272–73.

29. Kevin M. Watson, *Pursuing Social Holiness* (New York: Oxford University Press, 2014), 3.

30. Henderson, *A Model for Making Disciples*, 120.

31. Wesley, "A Plain Account of Christian Perfection," in *Works*, 433.

32. I adapted this model from Doug and Suzie Morrell, founders of Core Discipleship Ministries. We both share the belief that small groups of 3 to 5 are the most effective. Their website http://coregroups.org contains a host of information ranging from instructional downloads, discipleship material, and leaders guides, to name a few. The chart in Figure 1 was adapted from their website with permission.

33. See "John Wesley's Leadership Lessons," http://johnwesley leader.blogspot.com/2012/01/john-wesleys-3-strand-discipleship.html. (accessed 11 June 2015).

34. Henderson, *A Model for Making Disciples*, 130.

35. Frederick A. Norwood, ed., *The Doctrines and Discipline of the Methodist Episcopal Church, in America. With Explanatory Notes by Thomas Coke and Francis Asbury*, Facsimile ed. (Evanston, IL: The Institute for the Study of Methodism and Related Movements, Garrett-Evangelical Theological Seminary, 1979), 147 (henceforth, 1798 Doctrines and Discipline).

36. Their disagreement over God's election and man's freewill lasted their entire life. What is interesting is that before Whitefield died, he requested Wesley to preach at his funeral. Sugden records, "It was his own wish. 'If you should die abroad,' said Mr. Keen, 'whom shall we get to preach your funeral sermon? Must it be your old friend, the Rev. Mr. John Wesley?'....Whitefield answered, "Preach your fun."

    Wesley rarely preached on the Old Testament, but that day was an exception. He chose Numbers 23:10 as his text for the burial sermon, "Let me die the death of the righteous, and let my last end be like his." The message was filled with praise and adoration for the legacy Whitefield left behind. Obviously, the rift between them could not separate the deep respect they had for each other.

    See John Wesley, *John Wesley's Fifty-Three Sermons*, ed. Edward H. Sugden (Nashville: Abingdon Press, 1984).

37. Henderson, *A Model for Making Disciples*, 28.
38. Leonidas Rosser, *Class Meetings: Embracing Their Origin, Nature, Obligation, and Benefits* (Richmond, VA: Published by Author, 1855), 178.
39. J. W. Etheridge, *The Life of the Rev. Adam Clarke* (New York: Carlton and Porter, 1859), 189.
40. Holland Nimmons McTyeire, *A History of Methodism* (Nashville: Southern Methodist Publishing House, 1884), 204.

Chapter 7: A Comma That May Have Kept the Church in a Discipleship Coma

1. See James Price, *King James Onlyism: A New Sect* (Chattanooga, TN: James Price, 2006).
2. Larry Osborne, *Sticky Church* (Grand Rapids: Zondervan, 2008), 49.
3. Harold W. Hoehner, *Ephesians: An Exegetical Commentary* (Grand Rapids: Baker Academic, 2002), 549.
4. Bill Hull, *The Disciple-Making Pastor: The Key to Building Healthy Christians in Today's Church* (Grand Rapids: Revell, 1988), 54.
5. Ibid.
6. See my book *Growing Up: How to Be a Disciple Who Makes Disciples* (Bloomington, IN: CrossBooks, 2013).
7. Mike Breen, *Leading Kingdom Movements: The "Everyman" Notebook on How to Change the World* (Myrtle Beach, SC: Sheriar Press, 2013), (page not numbered).

Chapter 8: Making Disciples in a McChristian Culture

1. See https://www.bankofamerica.com/accessiblebanking/atm-banking-centers.go. The website boasts, "Do your banking from the comfort of your car with drive-through banking at selected locations. Allow additional time for mortgage and credit card payments to be processed."
2. "Carrie Fisher's Roles as Actress, Writer, and Daughter," *Entertainment Weekly*, http://www.ew.com/article/1990/09/28/

carrie-fishers-roles-actress-writer-and-daughter (accessed 15 July 2014).

3. Bill Hull, *The Disciple-Making Pastor: The Key to Building Healthy Christians in Today's Church* (Grand Rapids: Revell, 1988), 64.

4. Miles J. Stanford, *The Complete Green Letters* (1975; reprint, Grand Rapids: Zondervan, 1983), 6.

5. Ibid.

6. The book of Joshua identifies seven stone memorials in the land of Israel: Gilgal (4:20), Achan (7:26), King of Ai (8:28–29), Copy of the Law (8:30–32), Gibeon (10:27), Gilead (22:34), and Renewal of Covenant (24:26–27).

7. M. K. Hammond, *The Rabbi of Worms* (Eugene, OR: Wipf and Stock Publishers, 2013), 79.

8. I opted out of the group three weeks into the process because one of the men leading the charge insisted on implementing a one-on-one model. It was easier to leave the group than to change his mind.

9. Richard Foster, *Celebration of Discipline: The Path to Spiritual Growth* (New York: HarperCollins, 1978), 107.

Chapter 9: One for All, Not One at a Time

1. Some have wrongly believed this was the first filling of the Holy Spirit. John 20:22 records Jesus breathing upon the disciples in an upper room before saying, "Receive the Holy Spirit."

2. Eugene H. Peterson, *Traveling Light: Reflections on the Free Life* (Downers Grove, IL: InterVarsity Press, 1982), 182.

3. See N. T. Wright, *The Challenge of Jesus: Rediscovering Who Jesus Was & Is* (Downers Grove, IL: InterVarsity Press, 1999). Wright suggested that twelve men claimed to be the Messiah within 100 years prior to Jesus' coming and within 100 years after his death.

4. Here is an excerpt from *Growing Up* explaining the task Jesus completed: "What was the work Jesus was given to do? Many would argue that Jesus was talking about dying on the cross.

This, however, cannot be true, for His prayer preceded the cru-cifixion, and He could not then have described His work as hav-ing been accomplished. The context of the passage provides the correct answer. The work that Jesus was given to do was to train disciples. The Lord's Prayer in John 17 is a powerful discourse on disciple-making" (Bloomington, IL: Crossbooks, 2013), 102.

In *The Lost Art of Discipleship*, Leroy Eims states, "When you read the prayer carefully, you'll notice that He did not mention miracles or multitudes, but forty times He referred to the men whom God had given Him out of the world" (Grand Rapids: Zondervan, 1978, p. 28). Jesus invested in people, not programs. Yes, he spoke to the multitudes, but he spent his life with twelve men. Before leaving this earth, it was no coinci-dence that Jesus commanded his disciples to follow in his foot-steps by making disciples: "Go therefore and make disciples of all nations, baptizing them in the name of the Father and of the Son and of the Holy Spirit, teaching them to observe all that I have commanded you" (Matt. 28:19–20 ESV).

5. See Ed Stetzer and Eric Geiger, *Transformational Groups: Creating a New Scorecard for Groups* (Nashville: Broadman & Holman, 2014), Kindle Edition (Kindle Locations 200-202).
6. Ibid.
7. Matthew Henry, *An Exposition of the Old and New Testa-ments*, vol. 6 (Philadelphia: Haswell, Barrington, and Haswell Publishers, 1838), 840.
8. John Meier, *A Marginal Jew: Rethinking the Historical Jesus*, Anchor Bible Reference Library, vol. 3 (New York: Doubleday, 2001), 41–45.
9. Robby Gallaty, *Growing Up: How to Be a Disciple Who Makes Disciples* (Bloomington, IL: Crossbooks, 2013), 50.
10. James Strong, *Enhanced Strong's Lexicon* (Bellingham, WA: Logos Bible Software, 2001), μάρτυς.
11. See Gallaty, *Growing Up*, 14–15.
12. Babylonian Talmud, Taanit 7a. Quoted in Ann Spangler and Lois Tverberg, *Sitting at the Feet of Rabbi Jesus: How the*

Jewishness of Jesus Can Transform Your Faith (Grand Rapids: Zondervan, 2009), Kindle Edition (Kindle Location 1148).

Chapter 10: Roadblocks to Making Disciples

1. Thom Rainer and Eric Geiger, *Simple Church: Returning to God's Process for Making Disciples* (Nashville: Broadman & Holman, 2006), 113.
2. Bill Hull, *The Disciple-Making Pastor: The Key to Building Healthy Christians in Today's Church* (Grand Rapids: Revell, 1988), 72.
3. Brad J. Waggoner, The Shape of Faith to Come (Nashville: B & H Publishing Group, 2008), 12.
4. Mike Breen, *The Great Disappearance: Why the Word "Disciple" Disappears after Acts 21 and Why It Matters for Us Today* (eBook), Kindle Edition (Kindle Locations 263-264). (2013-03-27).
5. Billy Graham, *The Holy Spirit* (Waco, TX: Word, 1978), 147.
6. Edgar A. Guest, "Sermons We See" [Public domain], http://www.silverberch.com/guest.html (accessed 20 July 2014).

Chapter 11: Why You Can't Disciple an Unbeliever

1. Twitter, 9:27 am (accessed 19 January 2013), @derwinlgray.
2. This story was told to me by Don Wilton, pastor of First Baptist Church of Spartanburg, South Carolina.
3. Leonard Ravenhill, "Revival Hymn," http://www.revivalhymn.com/pdffiles/RevivalHymnTranscript.pdf [Internet] (accessed 24 March 2015).
4. Charles Studd, http://en.wikipedia.org/wiki/Charles__Studd [Internet] (accessed 24 March 2015).

Chapter 12: Can I Make Disciples?

1. Walter Bauer, A *Greek-English Lexicon of the New Testament and Other Early Christian Literature*, ed. Frederick W. Danker, 3rd ed. (Chicago: University of Chicago Press, 2000).

2. Franklin Graham, *Billy Graham in Quotes* (Nashville: Thomas Nelson, 2011), 155.

Chapter 13: MARCS of a D-Group

1. George H. Reavis, ed., and Joyce Orchard Garamella, illus., *The Animal School: The Administration of the School Curriculum with References to Individual Differences* (Peterborough, NH: Crystal Springs, 1999).
2. Spiros Zodhiates, *The Complete Word Study Dictionary: New Testament* (Chattanooga, TN: AMG Publishers, 2000). πιμπλημι
3. See Arturo Azurdia, *Spirit Empowered Preaching*. http://www.spiritempoweredpreaching.com/sermons.htm I heard Dr. Azurdia explain this concept when he visited New Orleans Baptist theological Seminary to speak in Chapel in 2005.
4. Dale Carnegie, *How to Win Friends and Influence People* (New York: Simon & Schuster, 1936), 55.
5. See Mack Stiles, *Evangelism: How the Whole Church Speaks of Jesus* (Wheaton, IL: Crossway, 2014).
6. My testimony is in the first chapter of *Growing Up: How to Be a Disciple Who Makes Disciples*.
7. Bill W. *My First 40 Years: An Autobiography by the Cofounder of Alcoholics Anonymous* (Center City, MN: Hazelden, 2000), 13–14. The interview was conducted in 1948.
8. Mike Breen, *Building a Discipling Culture*, rev. ed, (Pawleys Island, SC: 3DM Publishing, 2011), Kindle Edition (Kindle Locations 1184–1210). (2011-08-16).
9. D. A. Carson, *Love in Hard Places* (Wheaton, IL: Crossway, 2002), 61.
10. I heard Ed Stetzer make this comparison when he spoke at Brainerd Baptist Church in 2009.
11. Dietrich Bonhoeffer, *Life Together: The Classic Exploration of Life and Community*, trans. J. W. Doberstein (1937; San Francisco: HarperSanFrancisco, 1993), 110.

12. Ann Spangler and Lois Tverberg, *Sitting at the Feet of Rabbi Jesus: How the Jewishness of Jesus Can Transform Your Faith* (Grand Rapids: Zondervan, 2009), Kindle Edition (Kindle Locations 421-422). (2009-05-26).

13. For a process for studying, journaling, and memorizing the Word, check out my previous book, *Growing Up: How to Be a Disciple Who Makes Disciples* (Bloomington, IL: Crossbooks, 2013),

Conclusion

1. John R. W. Stott, *One Race, One Gospel, One Task*, World Congress on Evangelism, Berlin 1966; published in *Official Reference Volumes*, Volume 1, ed. Carl F. Henry and W. Stanley Mooneyham (Minneapolis: World Wide Publications, 1967), 46.

Appendix

1. Napoleon Hill, *Think and Grow Rich* (Minneapolis: Filiquarian Publishing, 1937; 1985), 108.

2. This section was adapted from Robby Gallaty, *Growing Up: How to Be a Disciple Who Makes Disciples* (Bloomington, IL: Crossbooks, 2013), 181–87.